Praise for *Loyalty Myths*

"*Loyalty Myths* is mandatory reading for anyone involved with customer relationship management initiatives and customer loyalty programs. Melding insights from the scholarly literature and real-life case studies, the authors cogently challenge conventional wisdom and offer valuable suggestions for understanding, building, and nurturing customer loyalty. A truly thought-provoking and fun-to-read book."

> —A. "Parsu" Parasuraman, James W. McLamore Chair,
> University of Miami, and editor of the
> *Journal of Service Research*

"Keiningham et al. have fired a full broadside at the "managerially correct" and seemingly unassailable notion that customer loyalty is all that matters. In examples including First Chicago, Tansaş, and Ryanair and through broadly researched data and analysis they show that knowing what customers want and will pay for is the issue. This is a great place to start when doing a full review of the effectiveness of your marketing spend to find advantage in your competitors' inabilities to differentiate themselves."

> —George Stalk, Senior Vice President of The Boston
> Consulting Group, and co-author of *Hardball:*
> *Are You Playing to Play or Playing to Win?*

"*Loyalty Myths* digs deep beneath the surface of conventional wisdom. It will make readers think twice about their longheld beliefs regarding customer loyalty management."

> —Ruth N. Bolton, W. P. Carey Chair in Marketing,
> Arizona State University, and former editor of the
> *Journal of Marketing*

"When something becomes a truism, it requires daring people to challenge it. In *Loyalty Myths*, Keiningham, Vavra, Aksoy, and Wallard undress 53 truisms of customer loyalty. By combining new research with real-life business practice, they document how accepted wisdom has misled managers in their pursuit of customer loyalty and profitability—strategies that in the worst case might put you out of business. Having made the reader painfully aware of the flaws in existing knowledge, the authors generously offer proven tactics that really work—strategies that will make your business succeed. It is my prediction that *Loyalty Myths* will become the next must read for successful business managers."

> —Tor W. Andreassen, Professor of Marketing,
> Norwegian School of Management

LOYALTY
MYTHS

LOYALTY MYTHS

Hyped Strategies That Will Put You Out of Business— and Proven Tactics That Really Work

Timothy L. Keiningham

Terry G. Vavra

Lerzan Aksoy

Henri Wallard

WILEY

John Wiley & Sons, Inc.

Published by John Wiley & Sons, Inc., Hoboken, New Jersey.

Published simultaneously in Canada.

Designations used by companies to distinguish their products are often claimed by trademarks. In all instances where the author or publisher is aware of a claim, the product names appear in Initial Capital letters. Readers, however, should contact the appropriate companies for more complete information regarding trademarks and registration.

No part of this publication may be reproduced, stored in a retrieval system, or transmitted in any form or by any means, electronic, mechanical, photocopying, recording, scanning, or otherwise, except as permitted under Section 107 or 108 of the 1976 United States Copyright Act, without either the prior written permission of the Publisher, or authorization through payment of the appropriate per-copy fee to the Copyright Clearance Center, Inc., 222 Rosewood Drive, Danvers, MA 01923, (978) 750-8400, fax (978) 646-8600, or on the web at www.copyright.com. Requests to the Publisher for permission should be addressed to the Permissions Department, John Wiley & Sons, Inc., 111 River Street, Hoboken, NJ 07030, (201) 748-6011, fax (201) 748-6008, or online at http://www.wiley.com/go/permissions.

Limit of Liability/Disclaimer of Warranty: While the publisher and author have used their best efforts in preparing this book, they make no representations or warranties with respect to the accuracy or completeness of the contents of this book and specifically disclaim any implied warranties of merchantability or fitness for a particular purpose. No warranty may be created or extended by sales representatives or written sales materials. The advice and strategies contained herein may not be suitable for your situation. You should consult with a professional where appropriate. Neither the publisher nor author shall be liable for any loss of profit or any other commercial damages, including but not limited to special, incidental, consequential, or other damages.

For general information on our other products and services or for technical support, please contact our Customer Care Department within the United States. at (800) 762-2974, outside the United States at (317) 572-3993 or fax (317) 572-4002.

Wiley also publishes its books in a variety of electronic formats. Some content that appears in print may not be available in electronic books. For more information about Wiley products, visit our web site at www.wiley.com.

Library of Congress Cataloging-in-Publication Data:

Loyalty myths : hyped strategies that will put you out of business—and proven tactics that really work / Timothy L. Keiningham [et al.].
    p. cm.
  ISBN-13 978-0-471-74315-6 (cloth)
  ISBN-10 0-471-74315-1 (cloth)
   1. Customer loyalty.   I. Keiningham, Timothy L.
  HF5415.525.L695   2006
  658.8'343—dc22

                                      2005006850

Printed in the United States of America.

10 9 8 7 6 5 4 3 2 1

To those who seek to make the world a better place and are crazy enough to believe that they actually can.

"Never doubt that a small group of thoughtful, committed citizens can change the world. Indeed, it's the only thing that ever has."

—Margaret Mead, anthropologist (1901–1978)

CONTENTS

MYTHS

Chapter 3: Loyalty Myths about Customers: Their Needs, Behaviors, and Referrals

Chapter 4: Loyalty Myths Concerning Loyalty Programs

PREFACE

We are committed to the belief that strategically directed and effectively nurtured customer loyalty can truly differentiate firms from their competitors and will generate sustained profits. Following the myths of loyalty, however, will almost surely cause firms and customers to suffer. By exposing the myths for what they are we all can win, business and customer alike—by simply being good to one another.

—Timothy L. Keiningham, Terry G. Vavra, Lerzan Aksoy, and Henri Wallard

Source: Cartoonybin.com. Reproduced with permission.

Loyalty! Without question, it is one of the greatest virtues humankind can possess. As renowned film producer Samuel Goldwyn once remarked, "I'll take fifty percent efficiency to get one hundred percent loyalty."[1] Like Goldwyn, most of us are willing to sacrifice much to achieve loyalty from those we depend upon.

So it is with management's current passion toward customer loyalty. CEOs worldwide consistently cite customer loyalty as one of if not *the* most important strategic objective of their firms. Billions of dollars are spent every year by firms pursuing increased loyalty from their customers. Over 40,000 books have been written espousing the virtues of customer loyalty and offering methods with which to accomplish it. Hundreds of thousands, perhaps millions of articles have been written worldwide describing the profit-healing benefits flowing from improved customer loyalty.

And why not? Doesn't every firm want loyal customers? The simple answer is, "Yes, but . . ." It is the "but" that is the problem. Because most of what we've been told about customer loyalty is just plain wrong. It isn't that there was a vast conspiracy designed to mislead the managers regarding the role of customer loyalty in business performance. The simple truth is that the science studying the subject was incomplete. "Incomplete" frequently tends to mean "wrong."

Scientific discovery—the basis of all true sciences—is based on incremental learning. Hypotheses and theories are forwarded, then tested, subjected to constructive scrutiny, and finally accepted or rejected. Casualties of reputation and pride often get caught up in this cycle. Professionals engaged in the development of a science have to accustom themselves to the inevitability that not all of their hypotheses or ideas will be right. The brightest thinkers of our times have been caught in such fallacious propositions. Theoretical physicist Stephen Hawking once proclaimed that cosmic black holes destroy the information of anything they ingest. Hawking's idea was later proved inaccurate and he admitted it.[2] Albert Einstein never accepted quantum theory, proclaiming, "I shall never believe that God plays dice with the world."[3] It seems, however, that God does indeed roll dice.

What many miss is that a scientific field progresses as much by negative proof as by positive proof. But the sophomore always hopes for positive outcomes—failure to find associations is somehow less proudly proclaimed than confirmed associations. Unfortunately, the most revered voices in a field are sometimes the most reluctant to point out their mistakes. (Big trees fall the hardest and are most resistant to challenge.) Such individuals often simply dig themselves deeper, ultimately dishonoring themselves and temporarily stymieing the evolution of their field.

So it is, we believe, in the current science of marketing with regard to the correct understanding of customer loyalty. Some thought leaders in this area seem reluctant to admit that their early ideas, while helpful in guiding further inquiry, were not completely accurate. We ourselves, the authors of this book, have committed similar sins. But we are not beyond admitting our misperceptions and moving forward. In a book about customer loyalty, it is probably best to remember the words of author Mark Twain, "Loyalty to petrified opinions never yet broke a chain or freed a human soul in this world—and never will."[4]

The subject of this book is the evolution of thinking about customer loyalty. The serious reader will have to set aside many of the platitudes she has previously learned—they simply don't work in today's marketplace! Our intention here is to offer, to the best of our current ability, a truer picture of how businesses can leverage customer loyalty to help them survive and succeed.

More important to each of the authors, our goal in writing this book is to quite literally change the world, or at least a piece of it. We have been fortunate to make our living by demonstrating that it is indeed *good business to be good to one another.* In a world where life's pressures make it easy for each of us to lose a piece of our humanity—our requisite civility to one another—it is sometimes easy for us to forget that fact.

The pursuit of customer loyalty can be a highly profitable strategy, but not by clinging to the myths that have developed surrounding the idea. Following the conventional wisdom that has been propagated about customer loyalty will almost surely cause firms large and small to suffer . . . which ultimately means that customers will suffer as well. If loyalty doesn't pay, then firms will have to pursue another strategy or they won't remain competitive. This book seeks to expose the myths for what they are so that in the end all of us win—by being good to one another.

The Myths of Loyalty: Did the Gods Mislead Us?

Source: Cartoonybin.com. Reproduced with permission.

Loyalty rules at every level. Loyal employees in any company create loyal customers, who in turn create happy shareholders.
                —Sir Richard Branson, Chairman, Virgin Group

[Loyalty] is a philosophy we live by at L.L. Bean, and one with which I couldn't agree more.
                —Leon A. Gorman, Chairman, L.L. Bean.

Loyalty "is the hidden force behind growth, profits, and lasting value"—the intangible that binds an organization together and manifests the strength and quality of its culture.[1]
                —Robert T. Herres, Chairman, USAA

T hese are strong words likely spoken with conviction and sincerity. But these leaders have been misled in their overwhelming reliance on loyalty as a panacea. They have been misled by a torrent of literature that monotonously reiterates false findings and wrongly advocates simple solutions. The marketing community has deified the early pioneers of loyalty, and these individuals have misled leaders (like those above) and followers alike who have honestly sought out good business strategy. Our goal is to set the record straight!

CHAOS IN PLEASANTVILLE

In what seems like only yesterday the consumer markets of the world operated with predictability and regularity. Customers could be depended upon to repeat-buy if they were at least minimally satisfied. Competitors were present, but they succeeded in luring only the occasional customer away; only infrequently did they become so aggressive as to openly solicit another's customers. Customers rarely drifted from their preferred brands.

Today, in the early twenty-first century, all of this has changed. Companies and brands today compete with a vengeance and do so in the most chaotic and hostile market ever faced by success-driven businesspeople. Maintaining market share has become extraordinarily difficult, and gaining more almost unthinkable. The old saying "You've got to run fast just to stay in place" has never been more true than in the resulting overcrowded product and service categories. Consumers have become beleaguered with a mind-boggling mass of offerings not just from competitors, but also from marketers as they extend their own brands or services. Take the venerable Oreo cookie: Once a single product on store shelves, today it's flanked by over 27 additional products bearing the Oreo brand! Each of these vies for customers' limited attention.

In this cacophonous market, products compete for recognition and purchase by a customer population that has become aggravatingly more fickle. But despite the increased indifference from customers, corporate boards and shareholders are no less demanding in their expectations for increased profits. These countervailing forces set up formidable odds for even the most creative businessperson. Pleasantville is no more.

FALSE IDOLS

It is within this contemporary battlefield that customer loyalty has become a favored competitive tool. This is, no doubt, a result of the countless promises made by the loyalty community concerning the benefits of loyalty as a business tactic. But so many of the mandates are fallacious. Take the rule that admonishes us to retain as many customers as possible, because the value of customers increases over time.

Let's examine this more closely. Businesspeople have come to acknowledge the impact of the "Pareto Principle" on the survival of their enterprises. Pareto, a late nineteenth century Italian economist and sociologist, recognized that a majority of his nation's wealth was held by a minority of the population. The Pareto Principle is also referred to as the 80–20 Rule, suggesting that 80 percent of the wealth was held by 20 percent of the population. This principle is widely substantiated in marketing data. Figure I.1 depicts a fictional product in which just 20 percent of the users generate 50 percent of the profits.

But as dire as Pareto's prescription is, the everyday reality is probably even more severe. It's likely (especially in services) that 60 percent of a business's customers could actually be generating negative profits—costing the business money! Given this fact, one can easily see how the mandate of keeping all the customers possible can actually be a recipe for disaster.

But why have loyalty advocates been so adamant in recommending that we keep all our customers? They've made a faulty presumption: that all customers get more valuable with age. This observation is a naïve one, based on a simplistic interpretation of customer cohort groupings.

To better understand the true state of affairs, consider the customers of a fictional business, Tim's Torpedo Tricycles, depicted in Figure I.2. Not all of Tim's customers are equally valuable. Some are good customers, generating substantial profits for the business. We'll call these customers *Desired Customers*. A second group contains customers who aren't technically unprofitable, but contribute near the

FIGURE I.1 Pareto Principle

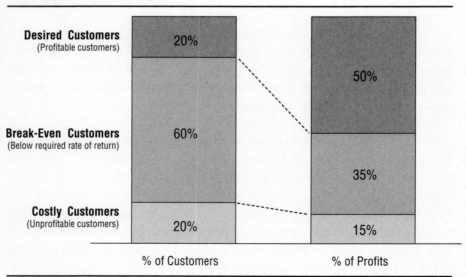

FIGURE I.2   Tim's Torpedo Tricycles

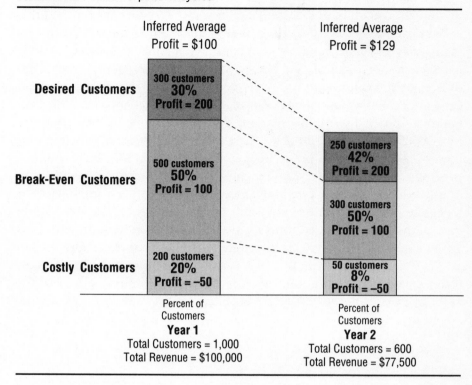

minimally accepted rate of return for the company. We'll call these customers, *Break-even Customers*. The third and final group contains customers who require substantial servicing that more than offsets their contribution. We'll call these customers *Costly Customers*.

If Tim's Torpedo Tricycles starts in year 1 with 1,000 customers, we'll arbitrarily assume as many as 300 could be desired customers—those from whom Tim can expect to make a decent profit. About 500 customers might be break-even customers, and as many as 200 might be costly customers.

Roll the clock forward one year. If only 600 of Tim's initial 1,000 total customers are left, the average profit per customer will *appear* to be higher. Have individual customers improved in their profit generation? It's highly unlikely.

What has probably happened is that Tim's *mix* of customers within the remaining 600 has significantly changed in the direction of the profitable customers. Costly Customers are more transient in nature, and many may have departed, looking for better deals. Of these unprofitable customers, only 50 Costly Customers remain. A smaller proportion of Break-even Customers have defected. Of the 500 original Break-even Customers, 300 remain. A majority of Tim's Desired Customers have remained; 250 of the original 300 are still active. Thus, in the remaining mix of 600 customers, Tim has a stronger concentration of valuable customers, yielding much richer average profits per customer ($129 to a previous $100). However, the increased yield of profit is not the result of individual customers becoming more valuable with tenure, but rather a change in the composition of Tim's customer population. This simple fact seems to have eluded most loyalty experts, even though numerous writers in various journals have sought to set the record straight.

As can be seen from this hypothetical example, retaining *all* customers wouldn't be a good idea for Tim's Torpedo Tricycles, nor for any business. But this has been the simplistic prescription. In contrast,

Source: Cartoonybin.com. Reproduced with permission.

allowing the profitable customers to leave would be an even worse idea. Consequently the real solution rests in knowing the value of each customer and then focusing loyalty efforts on those customers who are the most valuable.

This example underscores our proposition: Most current loyalty maxims are predicated on faulty data or on a superficial reading of longitudinal data. Yet businesspeople still believe loyalty to be the most effective strategy for competition in today's market.

Understanding that loyalty is a necessary marketing tool is, unfortunately, only a small step in the right direction. Executives face formidable odds in creating an effective loyalty program. Five marketplace megatrends exist that both sanction and yet challenge the employment of customer loyalty as an effective business tool.

The Epidemic of Customer Churn

The cable television and early cellular telephone industries were the first to notice the impact of customers enrolling for a service and then suddenly leaving, taking their business to another vendor. As this practice rose to epidemic levels, businesspeople in numerous other categories soon became aware of *customer churn*, started monitoring it, and began worrying about how to curtail it. Churn rates for some products and services have reached astoundingly high levels; they range from a trickle— 3 to 5 percent per year in categories like insurance—to a flood, with an attrition rate of 70 to 80 percent (such as consumers who switch from one mortgage provider to another at their next purchase occasion).

While customers are partially responsible, ironically businesses also engendered this fickle behavior. Industry practices to entice customers from a competitor by offering monetary incentives or promises of upgraded equipment have caused customers to understand the value of their patronage. This recognition has transformed customers into mercenary agents who are determined not to simply acquire a product or service, but to demand as much as possible for their patronage in the transaction.

As churn was acknowledged for the epidemic it was, loyalty became recognized as a logical cure. However, attempts to head off customer attrition have not always been well planned nor well executed.

FIGURE I.3   Churn Rates

Company	Retention Rate
USAA	96%–97%
State Farm	95%–96%
Standard insurance policy	85%–86%
1-800-CONTACTS	75%
General Motors	65%
Auto industry average	54%
Infiniti	35%
ABN AMRO Mortgage	20%–30%

Sources: Joe Kohn (2002), "Infiniti Looks to Build Sagging Customer Loyalty," *Automotive News*, January 21, 2002, p. 16; Caitlin Mollison, "ABN AMRO Mortgage Turns to Speech-Recognition Technology," *Internet World*, February, pp. 40–41; Jack Neff (2001), "Marketing 1000: Kevin McCallum," *Advertising Age*, October 8, S10; Frederick F. Reichheld, *The Loyalty Effect* (Boston, MA: Harvard Business School Press, 1996), pp. 250–251; Ernan Roman, "Customers for Life," *American Demographics*, July/August 1996, p. 66.

All too frequently, approaches to loyalty have been woefully inadequate or have been strategically naïve and misdirected. More troubling still, the planning has been predicated on fallacious promised benefits.

Attempts to minimize customer churn need to be better directed. Rather than using poorly thought-out tactics, businesses need to better understand their failure to provide strong, positive hooks for their customers. They need to examine their competition to determine how their customers are being so easily taken away. And switching incentives (disloyalty tactics), which ultimately backfire, need to be totally rethought.

Customer Behavior: Exclusivity Is Out, Divided Loyalty Is In

In what now seems like a fairy-tale marketplace, customers once dedicated themselves and their pocketbooks to a preferred brand, retailer,

Source: Cartoonybin.com. Reproduced with permission.

or supplier. On a superficial level, their behavior built trusting relationships with preferred vendors in exchange for preferential treatment. Psychologists tell us such behavior is really a way of coping with risk. Establishing relationships with preferred vendors helps customers reduce or eliminate six types of risk associated with buying products and services:

1. *Performance risk*—the risk that the product or service will not perform as expected/required/advertised.
2. *Psychological risk*—the risk that choosing the product or service will cause self-doubt or feelings of failure.
3. *Financial risk*—the risk that the product or service will not be worth its cost or not as economical as suggested.
4. *Safety risk*—the risk that the product or service will cause physical injury.

5. *Social risk*—the risk of condemnation by or embarrassment from friends or business associates for having chosen the product or service.
6. *Time risk*—the risk of consuming substantial time in selecting an alternative product or service (which may or may not be worth the effort).

Eliminating risk in customers' lives competes with another need, their need for novelty. Novelty is the pleasure of experiencing new products and establishing relationships with new vendors promising new outcomes and new experiences. Customers can be segmented on both their degree of willingness to undertake new risk and their need for or aversion to novelty. In general, and especially with higher-ticket items, more consumers will align themselves with controlling risk in their lives.

Unfortunately, there are also adverse consequences to dedicating oneself to a preferred vendor. Customers displaying dependent behavior can often feel a vendor may be taking advantage of them. Vendors have been known to raise prices for customers they consider captive. Vendors may also adopt a low service attitude toward customers they perceive as sure things, failing to recognize the need to continue to earn their customers' respect. Such disregard can ultimately erode the established relationship.

Customers subjected to such negligent treatment are likely to modify their behavior into a more self-serving posture, reasoning that they require backups in case their preferred vendor were out of stock or otherwise unable to meet their needs. This perspective has eroded the solitary relationships of the past and has given rise to more divided relationships.

In the market of the twenty-first century, customers are more likely to be loyal to a group of brands than to a single brand. This is particularly true if the chosen brand is the category leader and costs more. In contrast to the one-brand-for-life mentality of the past, today's consumers are blatant in their divided loyalties, cuckolding multiple brands for their own safety and pleasure.

Organizations need to acknowledge and understand this new be-

Source: Cartoonybin.com. Reproduced with permission.

havior. It calls for radically different strategies; some goals of the past are simply unrealistic today. No loyalty program or initiative should rely on customers' risk avoidance as a model for business success. Beyond the negative motive of risk avoidance, customers require a positive motive to create a positive brand preference.

Persistence versus Insistence

Customers' affinity for a particular product or brand is generally thought to be one of preference—a seeking of satisfactions previously delivered and received. In this scenario, the customer would willingly expend all necessary search time and willingly tackle substantial barriers to acquire a favored brand. This preference and search could properly be labeled as insistence for a specific brand. (As if understanding this, one of the first sociologists to write about customer loyalty, Melvin T. Copeland, actually labeled brand-prone behavior as *brand insistence*.[2])

In a contrary vein, there are industries today that capitalize on a quite opposite behavior. In the insurance business, customer retention or loyalty has been measured by how long customers *persist*. Persistence implies the need to overcome something—a negative motive. True brand loyalty is driven by positive motives reinforced by pleasant purchase experiences and products or services that perform as or better than expected. Unlikely as it might seem, many organizations delude themselves by interpreting customer persistence as true loyalty.

But the days are numbered for companies who rely on customer persistence. Customers simply aren't going to take it anymore! Every business entity needs to assure itself that its customers endure because of their desires for positive incentives. Barriers to switching or structural chains are not customer loyalty programs.

Source: Cartoonybin.com. Reproduced with permission.

Industry Boundaries and Other Constraints against Switching

Not all customers are able to travel freely among alternative brands or suppliers in a category. In some situations, customers must make a commitment to a particular equipment type or standard. Once this commitment is made, the costs of switching to a competitor (on another platform, for instance) become impractical and expensive. Companies may find themselves barred from appealing to certain customers who may have opted for a competing technology. Or a supplier may be unable to conduct business through a new channel that becomes attractive to some of its customers. Legal restrictions may also prevent appealing to certain classes or types of customers (for example, the liquor industry is rightfully prevented from exploiting the underage drinker market, despite the potentially high loyalty of such a segment).

Unfortunately, as statistics about customer retention and attraction are compiled, they are rarely qualified by the switching constraints and

Source: Cartoonybin.com. Reproduced with permission.

natural boundaries that may exist within many categories. Far too many companies pride themselves on high customer loyalty when in fact their existing customers are no more than hostages, eager to flee if only presented with an escape opportunity (i.e., a reasonable product or service alternative).

Businesses need to objectively examine the reasons for their customers' extensive tenure. Without such an examination, shackled purchasers may falsely be misconstrued as willfully loyal. Companies can't afford to rely on their customers' inertia to bond their business.

Lifetimes and Lifetime Values

Mainstream marketing has only recently discovered the concepts of customer lifetimes and lifetime values. Direct marketers originally created these concepts because they required metrics to justify the expense of finding and keeping customers. Using a time period or number of identifiable transactions as the average customer lifetime, direct marketers predict how long a new customer will remain a cus-

Source: Cartoonybin.com. Reproduced with permission.

tomer. The concept of customer lifetime also helps explain why some customers vanish after a certain number of purchase cycles.

Using lifetime value, direct marketers defend substantial investments in attracting and maintaining customers. By anticipating an annuity stream of purchases defined by lifetime value—the cumulative sum of profits (in current dollar values) expected to occur over the average customer lifetime—direct marketers can easily justify investing in a customer up to that amount.

Today, lifetime value has come to be recognized as one of the more critical criteria on which customers ought to be evaluated or scored. The resulting segments become the foundation of a truly effective customer loyalty initiative.

THE CRUSADE FOR LOYALTY

These five megatrends have created a marketplace of the early twenty-first century that is radically different from the past. In this market, yesterday's ideas and theories just won't cut it, so it is little wonder that businesses worldwide are searching for new tools with which to compete in order to survive and grow. In this environment, loyalty has become the business world's new nostrum. Pundits around the world have enshrined the concept, touting the miraculous benefits to be gained by improving net customer loyalty. The core premise maintains that by improving customer retention rates companies will not only curtail losses but will also radically boost their profits.

The most cited and perhaps most comprehensive discussion of this overly optimistic view is the 1990 *Harvard Business Review* article "Zero Defections: Quality Comes to Services."[3] This article boldly proclaimed that "companies can boost profits by almost 100 percent by retaining just 5 percent more [of their] customers. . . ." The article went on to extol the virtues of minimizing customer attrition: "Customer defections have a surprisingly powerful impact on the bottom line. They can have more to do with a service company's profits than scale, market share, unit costs, and many other factors usually associated with competitive advantage. . . . Low-defection strategies can overwhelm low-cost strategies." Rightly or wrongly, these bold promises easily gained the ear of executive suites around the world.

The idea that loyalty and profits walk in lockstep is a message that resonates with managers; it carries a message they want to believe. Establishing lower customer defection as an operating strategy also easily captured the imagination of management teams. When this article was first published, customer loyalty was rarely acknowledged as a business goal. Today, the evidence of the business community's eagerness to embrace loyalty is all around us. A quick search on Amazon.com for "loyalty" identifies an excess of 40,000 business books on the topic! Almost all of these books espouse the simple virtues of loyalty as a business strategy without reservation.

The exuberant way in which management has endorsed the potentials of customer loyalty can hardly be fathomed, let alone be overstated. A worldwide survey of CEOs conducted by the Conference Board in 2002 found that customer loyalty and retention was the most important challenge that the CEOs believed they faced—more important than improving stock performance, reducing costs, or developing leaders within their organizations.[4] Management's enthusiastic reception of this priority has resulted in a transformation in the way organizations are internally structured and managed, and how external interactions with customers are positioned and conducted.

The pursuit of customer loyalty has infiltrated management practice in numerous ways. Four of the most pervasive initiatives are:

1. Establishing interactive, tracking customer databases.
2. Adoption of large-scale customer relationship management (CRM) systems.
3. Embracing customer loyalty programs.
4. Creating and empowering customer call centers.

These initiatives dominate the infrastructure of current customer loyalty implementation and, like most infrastructure investments, they have consumed significant capital expenditures.

Has every company that commits to these activities been rewarded as promised? Hardly. Have most implementations been well directed? No. Are most sponsoring organizations benefiting from their investment? Only the exceptional ones. The fact is that most of the investments made to improve customer loyalty have been based on faulty assumptions and questionable findings and may therefore be considered a waste of money. In the next several sections we'll review examples where things came together in a fortuitous way—the "gods" of practice—and where things not only failed to come together but quite literally fell apart—the "goats" of practice.

Customer Database Gods

The corner grocery store owner of the 1940s and 1950s knew each of his customers—what they purchased on a typical visit; their preferences for quality and for brands. He courted his customers by establishing personal relationships and paying attention to what they purchased and why. Often he accomplished this personal service on the basis of nothing more than a sharp memory. Other times he kept crib notes on 3×5 cards carefully retained in a file or shoebox.

This merchant of simpler times bet that if he showed customers his appreciation of their business by paying attention to what they purchased, he could endear his establishment to them. Most customers appreciated the attention focused on their requirements and decisions; it simplified future shopping trips and made them feel comfortable with the store. In exchange, they rewarded the storekeeper with their continued and devoted patronage.

With the onset of mass distribution and the mass merchandisers it fostered, most small corner stores were made obsolete, but customers didn't forget the personalized service to which they had become accustomed. With the advent of computers in business, especially the personal computer, big business began to try to emulate the personalized attentions of the past. Because the mass merchandiser had thousands of customers and a large and transient labor force, the key to providing such service lay in the development of a customer database. In place of the storekeeper of yesterday, the computerized database served as the central memory.

Ironically, substantial databases already existed in some categories like department stores. Unfortunately, the vast potential of these databases was almost always circumscribed by their dedication to billing procedures; no attention had been paid as to how these databases might also be directed to identifying high-value customers and improving customer service in general.

Today marketing-oriented databases are becoming ubiquitous. In fact, it would be virtually impossible to find a firm of any size that would not claim to have one.[5] In order to better retain the customers a business wants, however, it must be able to identify them and understand their requirements.

Customer Database Goats

Simply having a marketing-oriented customer database isn't enough. It must first be made available throughout the organization; the customer database should be owned by everybody. Second, significant effort must be given to maintaining it. An out-of-date database is probably worse than no database at all.

One of the missions of a customer database is to strengthen the relationship a business or organization has with its customers. Certainly the airline industry's monitoring of passengers' flying miles exemplifies an attempt to recognize high-value customers. But if a database isn't maintained, or if marketing appeals are made to members of another database without first performing a "merge and purge" to reduce duplications, then unfortunate things can happen. While writing this book, one of the authors, a 33-year member of the American Marketing Association, received a solicitation from this organization to become one of its members! The obvious reaction: "Don't you know I'm a member?" And "Don't you care about my 33 years of membership?" This goof from marketing's own professional association!

CRM System Gods

Customer relationship management (CRM) is the label given to mining the information contained in company databases for building stronger relationships with customers in order to foster loyalty. The widespread adoption of CRM systems is one of management's most obvious concessions to nurturing customer loyalty. A recent Google search revealed in excess of 8.5 million hits for "CRM." (As a comparison, a Google search for "obesity" revealed only a third as many sites, 3.5 million.)

The basic operating objectives of CRM investments are twofold:

1. Data-mine the customer database to learn as much as possible about the purchasing habits and patterns of customers as possible. Use this information to better service and cross-sell customers.
2. Use the information for true segment-of-one marketing: offering the right product to the right customer at the right time with the right message, thereby increasing sales and customer loyalty.

The worldwide market for CRM systems is estimated to be anywhere from $35 billion to over $90 billion, depending upon how the

Source: Cartoonybin.com. Reproduced with permission.

reports define CRM. Regardless of the definition, it is a huge market, meaning a massive investment by firms in systems designed to get them close to their customers with the goal of improving customer loyalty.

CRM System Goats

Despite the attractive promise of CRM—the ability to sell the right product to the right person at the right time with the right message— for most firms the reality has not lived up to the hype. The subhead from a cover story in *CIO Magazine* entitled "The Truth about CRM" seems to say it all: "It's expensive, hard to implement, time consuming, and it may not work. It's time to forget the hype and take a hard look at the reality of CRM."[6]

> During the Thanksgiving holiday of 1998, Monster.com went live with a new CRM system. The goal of the Siebel Sales Enterprise system was to provide its telephone sales representatives with instant information on prospective customers, helping the company grow quickly around the world.
>
> Instead of facilitating business, the system became a gigantic nightmare. The system's response time was too slow to assist the telephone agents, and salespeople working in the field from laptops were totally locked out of the company's customer database! The problem continued for a year until Monster.com pulled the plug on the entire system. In the end, the system's failure cost Monster.com millions of dollars and consumed countless hours overcoming the initial problems and ultimately returning to the prior system.[7]

CRM systems don't have to fail in such a dramatic a way to be considered dysfunctional. A 2001 survey of senior marketing, sales, and customer service executives conducted by Cap Gemini found that 42 percent have no clue about their CRM initiative's return on investment (ROI).[8] Perhaps this reflects a desire to avoid bad news. By most estimates, CRM implementations have been nothing short of disastrous. Frequently costing tens or even hundreds of millions of dollars, most CRM programs have done next to nothing to add to the financial well-being of the firms who took the bait cast by CRM spokespeople. Here's the reality:

- The National Retail Federation's CRM conference survey of North American retail companies found that 69 percent gained little or no benefit from their CRM investments.[9]
- According to the Gartner group, around 50 percent of U.S. and more than 80 percent of European CRM projects are failures.[10]
- *CRM: Pitfalls & Potential* (by analysts at the Butler Group) estimates that 70 percent of all CRM implementations fail.[11]

To quote one Booz-Allen principal, Peter Grambs, "It's pretty endemic out there that there is a lack of satisfaction with CRM programs to date. . . . People are reticent to say, 'My $100 million dollar project is a failure.' But when you're looking for returns, you can see they're not there."[12]

Loyalty Program Gods

The other obvious change in management practices in the pursuit of customer loyalty is the ubiquitous loyalty programs offered by firms throughout North America and Europe (and, given current growth rates, soon to be the same in Australia). For example:

- More than 76 percent of all U.S. grocery retailers with 50 or more stores now offer a frequent shopper program; 53 percent of U.S. grocery customers are enrolled in such programs.[13]
- Half of the 10 largest retailers in the United States and the United Kingdom in each of the seven major retail categories have launched loyalty programs.[14]
- Eighty-nine million people are members of airline frequent flyer programs in the world; 74 million frequent flyer members reside in the United States.[15]

- Forty percent of all Visa and MasterCard issuers operate a rewards program tied to their credit card offering.[16]

- Forty-five percent of all U.S. and Canadian small business owners belong to a loyalty program sponsored by one of their suppliers. Of these, 60 percent belong to more than one program, with the average participation exceeding 2.3 programs.[17]

In fact, total U.S. consumer membership in customer loyalty programs stood at approximately one billion members in 2004.[18] This is an average of more than four programs per U.S. adult. In Canada, 70 percent of all households participate in at least one loyalty program.[19] Clearly, the global market for customer loyalty programs is immense and has already been significantly exploited.

Source: Cartoonybin.com. Reproduced with permission.

Loyalty Program Goats

Multi-merchant loyalty coalitions now exist virtually everywhere—in Canada, Argentina, Peru, Singapore, Poland, Germany, Australia, Malaysia, Thailand, Norway, Turkey, El Salvador, and the Philippines, to name a few. Their very acceptance caused them to be "hoisted by their own petard."

The proliferation of loyalty programs tends to homogenize otherwise indistinguishable operations even more by minimizing opportunities for meaningful differentiation. As a result, customers perceive equivalence among various loyalty programs and, even worse, are becoming bored with the programs. Research into hotel frequent guest programs found that once the branding and logos were removed from the rewards catalogues, members failed to recognize differences between competing programs.[20] Further, 19 percent of loyalty program members claim that they usually forget about the loyalty program points they have earned and therefore their points expire before being used. And among customers currently not participating in a loyalty program, 47 percent had no interest in joining one in the future.[21] "The problem of ubiquity resides not only in the proliferation of loyalty programs in the marketplace, but also in the stunning sameness of the reward offerings of most programs. Across industries, consumer fatigue and boredom appear to be directly tied to the unimaginative redemption choices found in most reward catalogs: the ho-hum 'toaster-style' awards, discount offers from the 'usual suspects,' anemic cash-back offers, magazine subscriptions or gift certificates from the same half-dozen Internet retailers. Even airline miles have lost some of their luster, with miles becoming more difficult to redeem in the middle of a prolonged travel recession."[22]

If programs are perceived as ever-present and effectively identical, their ability to generate a positive ROI is virtually zero. Worse still, retailers that have instituted loyalty programs frequently fail to account for all the costs associated with their programs. A McKinsey study found the following:[23]

▪ Sixteen major European retailers had $1.2 billion tied up in annual discounts to customers. Several supermarket chains were allotting in excess of $150 million annually.

▮ For large retailers, when accounting for all costs (training, marketing, IT, fulfillment, etc.), investment can reach $30 million in the first year; annual maintenance costs can reach $5 million to $10 million thereafter.

▮ For a retailer to break even on the cost of rewards alone, sales would have to increase by 6 percent on average. The gains of the earliest U.S. and European retailers to offer loyalty programs averaged 1 to 3 percent in groceries, and 5 to 8 percent in department stores during the first year; later loyalty program entrants eroded even these moderate sales gains.

Are loyalty programs becoming modern-day versions of S&H Green Stamps, a staple of American shopping in the mid twentieth century and possibly the first loyalty program? (For readers too young to remember, grocery stores used to give green stamps at checkout. Customers would then paste them into books, and redeem the books for merchandise at S&H redemption centers.) The answer for most programs would appear to be a resounding *yes*, only the infrastructure, marketing, and fulfillment costs of today's programs has made them a deep money pit.

Call Center Gods

The overarching mission to build loyalty has demanded that firms find ways to remain ever more accessible to their customers and, where sought, to create dialogues with them. The leading management weapon of choice has been the call center. Contact (call) centers have become one of the most prevalent means for companies to interact with their customers. For many firms, such as airlines, credit card companies, and hotels, call centers provide the *primary* communications link between customers and organizations.

This has required companies (and government and emergency services) to reengineer their infrastructures to handle increasingly knowledge-intensive, data-driven operations. It has meant evolving the low-tech customer service centers of yesterday into high-tech, multichannel, touch-point operations (for example, e-mail, fax, mail, kiosk, and Internet). Industries and individual companies are switching on to this perspective. *Best's Review* reports on a movement within the insurance industry to champion customer interaction centers (CICs).[24] The objective of these CICs is to provide superior and differentiated service through channel flexibility and by integrating customer-specific information resident in disparate databases throughout the enterprise. An editorial in the *Harvard Business Review*, "Don't Take Calls, Make Contact," reiterates the importance of this message.[25]

According to call center expert Jon Anton, "[The] ease of customer access is fast emerging as the critical element of a global customer relationship management (CRM) strategy. In the not too distant future, customers will deal preferentially with those companies that are deemed to be the most accessible. Even CRM can easily be defined in terms of access to information: CRM is the seamless accessibility by internal and external customers to their mission-critical company information by the integration of a company's telephone system, web site, and e-mail touch-points, resulting in satisfying customer self-service for initial product purchases, followed by targeted intelligent up-sells and cross-sells, and finally the *creation of customer loyalty*, value, and profitability."[26]

Not surprisingly, there has been explosive growth in the number of call centers worldwide within the last decade, to the point where they now represent a significant factor in both North American and European economies. In 2001 there were 55,800 call centers in North America, of which 90 percent (or 50,200) were located in the United States. In 1999, the U.S. Bureau of Labor Statistics estimated that 1.55 million agents worked at call centers in the United States alone—more than 1.4 percent of private-sector employment.[27] This figure is similar in Europe, where the European Union reports 1.2 percent of its working population employed in call centers. By far, however, the largest call center market in Europe is in the United Kingdom, where the call center percentage of employment is a whopping 2.2 percent.[28]

And with this new customer-to-firm communications option, customers are definitely taking the opportunity. In 1998, AT&T reported that 40 percent of its more than 260 million daily calls were toll-free. It seems highly likely that a significant percentage of these 104 million daily toll-free calls ended up at some firm's call center.[29]

Thank you for calling the All-American Computer service line. Due to current call volume, your estimated wait time is 35 minutes. We appreciate your understanding, as it is currently after midnight in India.

Source: Cartoonybin.com. Reproduced with permission.

Call Center Goats

The rapid growth of the call center industry has resulted in numerous research studies, most of which have focused on operational issues associated with efficient call center management.

Research regarding call centers, customer satisfaction, and customer loyalty has been much less explored. The little research that does exist finds that customers are less satisfied with call center operations than they are with more traditional office-based (in-person) services. Furthermore, researchers have found that virtually all of the metrics used to manage call centers are not positively correlated to customers' levels of satisfaction. Numerous newspaper and magazine articles support these findings. As a recent *Fortune* magazine article lamented, "Companies worldwide are installing telephone support systems as a way to save money, and to help serve their clients faster. But the customer experience can be far from fast—or helpful."[30]

Delta Airlines Looks Offshore to Save Money

Delta Air Lines, Inc. has been losing money since the terror-ist attacks on Sept. 11, 2001, and doesn't anticipate returning to profitability anytime soon. But it's getting some relief by outsourcing parts of its call-center operations offshore. The strategy is expected to save $26 million this year. Now a portion of some 91 million calls per year are answered in India and the Philippines. Delta will sign with a third (In-dian) vendor in the coming weeks.

Because call-center employees are often the first con-tact with customers, Delta includes "accent neutralization" as part of its training to help reduce communication problems.[31]

Delta to Close India Call Center

Financially troubled Delta Air Lines Inc. said Wednesday it was shuttering one of its three call centers in India, but declined to discuss whether the move was related to a survey asking cus-tomers if they would be willing to pay a fee to speak to a U.S.–based agent rather than one in India. Outsourcing is rela-tively unusual in the airline industry. Chicago–based United Air Lines Inc. and Fort Worth, Texas–based American Airlines have call centers overseas, but those centers are staffed with company employees.[32]

WHERE ARE THE HAPPY, LOYAL CUSTOMERS?

Too often, good ideas fail because managers are not willing to invest both their capital and personal commitment. However, as we've docu-mented, the same accusations can't be leveled at customer loyalty ini-tiatives. Firms have spent a great deal of money on systems designed to enhance customer loyalty. It would be hard to believe that the loy-alty-building failures identified with CRM, loyalty programs, and call centers are the result of a lack of management support (either leader-ship or financial); managers have clearly stepped up to the plate and adopted the loyalty doctrine.

Given management's sincere goals and willingness to invest, we would expect to see a world of happy, loyal customers—and given the promise of customer loyalty, we should also expect steady increases in business performance. So what is the reality? If national satisfaction indices are any guide, we are not seeing large-scale numbers of highly satisfied customers. In fact, looking at data from the American Customer Satisfaction Index (ACSI) run by the University of Michigan, one would be hard pressed to say that customers would rate their level of satisfaction better than a grade of C. Since 1994, the first year that the ASCI was conducted, customers' satisfaction levels have ranged between a 70 and 75: not exactly a ringing endorsement of an outstanding relationship with the firms with whom they conduct business.

Given the intense focus of managers on improving customer loyalty, we would also expect to see a measurable change in brand loyalty. And indeed we have, but not in the direction we would want or expect.

▮ Consumers view low price as more important than brand name in 28 of 37 product categories; in six categories, price and brand are essentially equal; only in three categories—automobiles, liquor, and beer—is brand name more important than price.[33]

▮ One in five items sold in U.S. stores is now a store brand, while in Europe that figure is two in five items. Forty-five percent of shoppers in 2001 stated that they are more likely to switch to a store brand, up from 31 percent in 1996.[34]

▮ Seventy-nine percent of casual apparel customers and 70 percent of grocery customers state that they are always seeking alternatives to their current retailers.[35]

Considering this incredible decline in brand loyalty, it is easy to understand management's rabid adoption of customer loyalty programs as the remedy. Unfortunately, the results are clear: Despite all the time and money spent to enhance loyalty, customer loyalty is more difficult to find than ever.

SETTING THE RECORD STRAIGHT

While most database initiatives, CRM and loyalty efforts, and call center programs do not live up to their promise, it should be noted that they are not inherently faulty. Nor are many of the other tactics used to generate loyalty in and of themselves wrong. They have simply been built on overgeneralized maxims. The problem for managers is that even if all the tenets upon which these and other loyalty tactics were implemented proved to be true, successful implementation of any process designed to build customer loyalty on a large scale would prove daunting.

Customer loyalty as a business strategy is incredibly seductive. It fits perfectly with our sense of justice and fair play. We want to believe that good behavior leads to good outcomes—simply put, it is good business to be good. And a loyalty metric would seem an objective and perfect fit for such a noble (and, we believe, ultimately correct) business truism. However, many of the propositions used to create and support today's loyalty strategies just aren't correct. Most are patently false, making their prescriptions financially dangerous. But as nineteenth-century social critic Alexis de Tocqueville observed, "The public will believe a simple lie rather than a complex truth." That dictum could well have been written about the myths of customer loyalty.

The difficult truth regarding customer loyalty is that how it links to growth and profitability is far more complex than we have been led to believe. A blind pursuit of customer loyalty is at best a case of misallocated resources. But at worst it is a recipe for financial disaster.

In the following chapters, we identify the misunderstandings surrounding the application of loyalty. But beyond identifying the pitfalls, in a summary chapter we describe the correct way to benefit from loyalty practices. By disposing of the myths surrounding loyalty, we hope to stimulate a proper focus on customer loyalty. We are committed to the belief that loyalty can truly differentiate firms from their competitors and generate sustained profits. Our belief is that the golden rule of business *can* be that it *is* good business to be good. Treating customers and employees with decency and respect can pay substantial dividends.

CHAPTER 1

Loyalty Myths That Subvert Company Goals

Source: Cartoonybin.com. Reproduced with permission.

*Since we became a public company, we've had the highest reten-
tion of customers in the industry . . . we are not going to surrender
that leadership position.*[1]

> —John Chapple, Chairman, CEO, and President,
> Nextel Partners, Inc.

N o industry provides a better example of the misconception of
customer loyalty as a pervasive corporate goal than the banking
industry.

The 1990s was a decade of great turmoil for the U.S. banking industry. Competition was emerging from a host of new, nonbank businesses that were cherry-picking some of the retail banks' most
profitable lines of business. Customers were beginning to be allowed
to write checks on money market accounts obtained through their
brokers, arrange auto financing through automobile manufacturers,
buy annuities through their insurance agents, and obtain credit cards
from credit card–only financial institutions operating nationally. At the
same time, interstate banking was coming into existence, guaranteeing
that larger national banks would begin to compete in what were previously relatively local or regional markets.

Not surprisingly, banks were desperately seeking a solution for
increasingly tighter profit margins. In a 1991 *Journal of Retail Banking*
article, Frederick Reichheld (a loyalty advocate we've previously mentioned) and Bain & Company colleague David Kenny prescribed the
following remedy:

> Neither cost savings nor price increases will solve the
> branch profitability problem. To build sustainable profits,
> banks must "grow" deposits cost-effectively. And about the
> only way to do so is by raising customer retention rates.[2]

Reichheld and Kenny were by no means lone voices addressing
the U.S. banking industry during this time. In fact, the Bank Marketing

Association (BMA) and its affiliate trade journal, *Bank Marketing*, were overflowing with appeals to compete on service for enhanced customer loyalty. The BMA was so convinced of the importance of loyalty in solving banks' profitability problems that in 1989 it established a separate organization, the Quality Focus Institute, with the stated aim of achieving "greater customer satisfaction and retention."[3]

THE PARABLE OF THE COSTLY CUSTOMER: FIRST NATIONAL BANK OF CHICAGO

During the early 1990s, First National Bank of Chicago (now Banc One) would definitely have been classified as suffering profitability problems. Despite having the largest market share in the Chicago area and the greatest reach of any Chicago institution, the bank's return on equity was a pathetic 5 percent, compared to the industry benchmark of 15 percent. To combat the problem, the company named Jerry Jurgensen, a former First Chicago CFO, to head the community banking group in 1993. As a numbers man, Jurgensen did not dodge the company's earnings problems. "First Chicago's profitability as a retail bank is a problem. It needs to earn more, there's no question about it."[4]

One of the first things that First Chicago did under Jurgenson's supervision was to examine the profitability of its customer base. What they found was not pleasant: only one-third of the customer base was generating an adequate return. The search for distinguishing characteristics between its profitable and unprofitable customers revealed that the profitable segment was more accustomed to using the self-service channels the bank offered. In a concurrent review, the bank examined the costs associated with its operations. It determined that interactions with its branch tellers were one of the most costly means of delivering its routine banking services. ATM and banking by telephone (the primary modes of self-service) were obviously far more cost effective. Weighing the costs of servicing its different customer groups, the bank resolved to persuade some of its low-balance customers to use the less costly interaction modes. As a result, on April 25, 1995, First Chicago announced that it would begin to charge some low balance checking customers $3 if they sought teller assistance (for transactions that could have been completed through an ATM or by bank-by-phone). "If they change their behavior, it's a win-win," Jurgensen said. "And if they don't, at least they're paying fairly for the way they use the bank."[5]

Not surprisingly, the public outcry was immediate and merciless. Magazine and newspaper articles excoriated First Chicago's decision. Some of the resulting headlines included:

"Thanks for Your Deposit. That'll Be $3" (*Business Week*, May 15, 1995).[6]

"Tack on $3 for that Trip to the Bank Teller" (*Chicago Tribune*, April 26, 1995.)[7]

"Fees from Hell: How Fiendish Is Your Bank?" (*Money*, July 1995).[8]

"Need a Teller? A Big Bank Plans $3 Fee" (*New York Times*, April 27, 1995).[9]

Other media joined the criticism, including the late humorist Erma Bombeck in an article entitled "Our Friendly Bankers Have Become Greedy Thieves."[10] Jay Leno's opening monologue on NBC-TV's *Tonight Show* skewered First Chicago. Leno's punch line: "For $3 you can talk to a human teller, and for $4, they'll talk dirty to you."[11]

Politicians and consumer groups leaped at the opportunity to denounce the bank. Representative Maxine Waters (D-CA) called for a boycott of the bank.[12] Waters and Joseph Kennedy (D-MA), both members of the House Banking Committee, threatened to postpone legislation to expand banking powers because of the banking community's seeming disregard evidenced by the fee.[13]

Competitors quickly moved to take advantage of the situation with advertisements lampooning the fee in aggressive attempts to woo First Chicago's customers. Harris Bancorp took out a full-page advertisement in the *Chicago Tribune* assuring "free and unlimited access to our tellers."[14] First Illinois Bank's advertisement declared: "There's no such thing as a $3 bill."[15] In yet another ad, under a photo of a bank teller, MidCity Financial Corporation's ad proclaimed, "At our banks, this is not an endangered species."[16] And another bank's television advertisement had a confused customer approaching a bank window and asking, "Are you a teller?" The response: "Yes, that will be $3 please."[17]

From the sublime to the ridiculous, several Chicago-area banks actually paid customers who visited teller windows.[18] Lake Forest Bank Trust Co. gave $3 to customers after their transactions were finished. Harris Bancorp gave out $1 bills to customers who asked if it charged teller fees. Northview Bank & Trust offered a $3 rebate for new accounts that required a teller transaction. And First American Bank offered $10 to customers for switching from First Chicago, supporting the offer with print ads questioning, "Why pay to bank there when we'll pay you to bank here?"

Competitors' cash incentives were hardly the only inducements for customers to switch banks in the wake of First Chicago's decision. An *American Banker* article reported that Chicago-area banks, in general, averaged less in fees than First Chicago per $100 of deposits.[19] Survey research conducted that same year for *U.S. Banker* magazine among depositors suggested that First Chicago's approach was guaranteed to erode loyalty to the bank. Nearly 54 percent of participants in the survey said that they would change banks if required to pay a $3 teller fee. First Chicago officials did admit to losing hundreds of checking customers (although they kept the exact number proprietary).[20] Examination of Federal Deposit Insurance Corporation data clearly showed that First Chicago's average deposits per branch declined following the initiation of the new teller fee plan. (See Figure 1.1.)[21]

First Chicago's approach was far from a conventional customer retention strategy. Ruth Susswein, then executive director of the consumer group Bankcard Holders of America, disparaged the difference between most banks' stated focus on building loyalty and First Chicago's fee-for-service strategy. "On one hand, banks are saying they want relationship banking so that consumers can do all their banking at one institution," she noted. "But on the other hand, they are tearing the relationship apart by tacking on all these 'nuisance fees.' What are customers getting if they can't go to a teller anymore?"[22] And given Reichheld and Kenny's assertion that for banks "about the only way to build sustainable profits" is "by raising customer retention rates,"[23] Jurgensen's strategy should have sent First Chicago into a death spiral. What exactly did happen?

FIGURE 1.1 Average Deposits at First Chicago

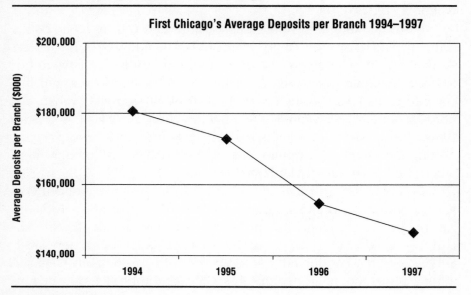

First Chicago's Average Deposits per Branch 1994–1997

Source: FDIC Online.

In the first full month following the announced charges, self-service ATM transactions at First Chicago doubled, and then increased an additional 50 percent a year later. Teller transactions dropped by one-third. By the end of 1995, more than 80 percent of depositors' transactions were being conducted electronically, and more than two-thirds of all account deposits were being made through ATMs or automated clearing houses (ACH).[24]

As a result, the bank made an adequate return on 44 percent of its customers (compared to only 33 percent before the change) and profits jumped 28 percent![25] Most observers were forced to admit that First Chicago's unorthodox approach to customer relationships had been highly successful. The title of a 1996 *Journal of Retail Banking Services* article summed up the general consensus: "First Chicago's Account Realignment Succeeds."[26]

It would be hard to find a more poorly received and seemingly anti-loyalty strategy than that of First Chicago's introduction of teller fees. Clearly it was designed to change customer behavior (either through the use of less expensive bank channels, or by encouraging customers to leave the bank), but First Chicago's success is also a testimony to the fallacy of loyalty myths as they influence and confuse company goals. Around the time that First Chicago was raising its profitability by instituting what most would consider an anti-loyalty strategy, the Bank Marketing Association was closing down its Quality Focus Institute because of a distinct lack of success stories and the corollary growing disillusionment among member banks at the lack of returns forthcoming from traditional customer loyalty initiatives.[27]

Jay Leno and others may have gotten the first laugh, but First Chicago laughed last and laughed best.

The Moral of the Costly Customer

To be profitable, businesses don't always have to blindly follow the folklore that urges the wholesale retention of all customers. A business should first understand which of its customers are profitable for it and

Source: Cartoonybin.com. Reproduced with permission.

why. Then it's appropriate to incent customers to engage in behaviors that are economically beneficial for the business. Just as was the case in the U.S. banking industry of the 1990s, ill-conceived customer loyalty objectives tend to pervade many companies' corporate goals today. The myths driving this orientation have become folklore in corporations worldwide and are so widely believed that they've been virtually unchallenged—until now. In contrast, organizations like First Chicago who aren't afraid to challenge myths have helped alert the marketing community to the fact that not all of the loyalty mandates from the so-called experts necessarily apply to their business, nor lead the way to greater profits.

LOYALTY MYTH 1: The Number One Goal of Any Firm Should Be Customer Loyalty

In 1960, Theodore Levitt wrote "Marketing Myopia," one of the most widely-quoted and reprinted *Harvard Business Review* articles.[28] The article warned of the dangers from firms shortsightedly focusing on their products and, in doing so, overlooking the needs of their customers. Levitt insisted, "the organization must learn to think of itself not as producing goods or services but as buying customers, as doing the things that will make people want to do business with it."

Without question, Levitt was absolutely correct. Firms exist to satisfy customer needs and wants and survive only by doing so. During the time of Levitt's article, however, many firms had lost sight of why they existed, arrogantly believing that "the market will buy whatever we choose to sell." This was during the same era that Japanese auto manufacturers were making inroads into the U.S. market by listening to consumers' concerns and building smaller vehicles. U.S. auto manufacturers continued to churn out large, gasoline-guzzling vehicles not because of their inability to make smaller cars, but because the profit margins were significantly higher on larger vehicles.

The world has changed a lot since then. Today most managers recognize that losing sight of customer needs is a recipe for disaster, though we might argue about how their firms actually address these needs.

Levitt's words still ring true, however. The problem is how the misinterpretation of Levitt's maxim has evolved in the modern era, which can loosely be summarized "customer loyalty is the number one goal of any firm." Though the emphasis may be exaggerated, business news stories demonstrate that the message is often forgotten. It is not difficult to find articles like the following:

- "Broke But Beloved," which begins "Say this for WINfirst, the troubled cable, telephone and Internet provider: It has very loyal customers. Since filing for Chapter 11 bankruptcy protection in March . . ."[29]

- "Loyal Following Couldn't Keep Jacksonville, Mich.–Based Jacobson's Going."[30]

- "Garden Botanika, Inc., the Redmond-based cosmetics and personal care products company, announced today it has filed a voluntary petition under Chapter 11 of the United States Bankruptcy Code. . . . Garden Botanika remains an industry leader with high sales and extremely loyal customers."[31]

Source: Cartoonybin.com. Reproduced with permission.

In fact, many of the dot-com disasters could have reported similar results: loyal customers but no profits.

The fundamental purpose of any business is to identify and satisfy customer needs at a profit, an idea Theodore Levitt certainly embraced. The problem is that customer loyalty *can be purchased*, and frequently is! But to paraphrase an old saw, "You can't buy things for a dollar, sell them at 99 cents, and make up the difference in volume!"

LOYALTY MYTH 2: Firms Should Emphasize Retention Efforts Rather than Acquisition Activities

The underlying logic of this myth rests on the trade-off between the costs of acquiring new customers and the costs of maintaining current ones. Conventional wisdom (seeded by the maxim "It costs less to retain a current customer than to win a new one") suggests that, all other things being equal (which is most often not the case), your odds are greater of receiving some return from investing in a current customer rather than chasing a potential one. This myth is further fueled by the beliefs that customers purchase more as their lifetimes lengthen (promising even greater than linear returns) and that they help recruit additional customers through positive word of mouth. Because marketing departments have traditionally overspent on advertising and have underspent on retention, the message also carries some novelty.

Even if the underlying reasoning were correct (which it is not, as will be demonstrated later in this book), it is ridiculously simplistic. Attracting and retaining customers are *both* critical processes. Economic success cannot be achieved by focusing exclusively on customer retention to the detriment of attracting new customers. Even with an ardent focus on retention, customers will defect and will need to be replaced. Therefore, a blind adherence to this myth will be nothing short of disastrous.

The most obvious flaw in this misconception is its complete disregard for the product life cycle (PLC). There are four generally accepted stages in a product's life cycle: introduction, growth, maturity/saturation, and decline.[32] A typical PLC pattern is depicted in Figure 1.2. Firms operating in each of these various phases have dif-

FIGURE 1.2   Product Life Cycle

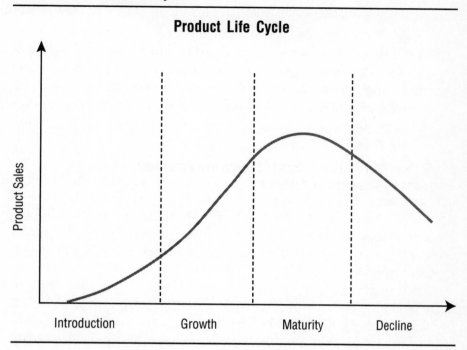

ferent strategic objectives that weigh heavily on the cost of acquisition versus retention.

1. **Introduction:** With the launch of a new product, success hinges on building a critical mass of early adopters. In this stage, product awareness and acceptance are the key strategic objectives.

2. **Growth:** The product is now accepted by the larger market, so consumer demand increases and the market expands. In this stage, brand awareness and market share are the key strategic objectives.

3. **Maturity/Saturation:** The market for the product has reached saturation. Growth comes largely at the expense of competitors,

and therefore competition becomes intense. In this stage, defending market share and maximizing profits are the key strategic objectives.

4. Decline: Sales decline as the product becomes out-of-date or out of fashion. In this stage, firms must decide on one of three strategic objectives: (1) rejuvenate the product with new features/functions; (2) "harvest" the product (reduce costs and continue to sell to a loyal niche segment); or (3) discontinue the product.

Therefore, the best thing that can be said about myth 2 is that, like a broken clock, it is correct at some times of the day. When firms are in the introductory and growth phases of their offerings, customer acquisition is critical. Conversely, when products are in the maturity and decline phases, customer retention takes on much greater importance.

Firms ignore the differing strategic objectives of the product life cycle at their peril. We need only look to Apple computer to be reminded of this. Apple popularized the computer by making it available to the masses through the introduction of the Apple II in 1977, established a computer and operating system that made the computer usable by nontechnical people through the introduction of the Macintosh in 1984, and was the first to commercialize the laser printer. These innovations resulted in explosive growth in the market for computers, printers, and software. As a result, Apple grew quickly and profitably. But its growth rate was far less than the growth of the market, as Apple was content with having a highly loyal but small customer base.

Apple disdained Microsoft's mass marketing strategy in favor of maintaining its highly profitable and opinionated market niche. "The only problem with Microsoft is that they just have no taste," Steve Jobs, Apple's co-founder, lamented. "They don't think of original ideas, and they don't bring much culture into their products."[33] This observation reveals a serious strategic blunder. While Apple computer users remain fiercely loyal, the firm's market share of computers and the operating systems that run them is relatively small, diminishing its ability to influence the market. There was even a time in the mid-1990s when Apple's ability to survive was in doubt. Fortunately, long-time adversary Microsoft Corporation and its chairman, Bill Gates, saved Apple with a $150 million investment. Apple had had the opportunity to be the dominant player in this market; that title now resides with Microsoft.

LOYALTY MYTH 3: Companies Should Strive to Make All of Their Customers Attitudinally and/or Behaviorally Loyal

The fundamental assumption underlying this myth is that all customers are or can be made to be profitable for a firm. An examination of customer profitability invariably reveals that while organizations will always have some highly profitable customers, they are also likely to have some highly unprofitable customers. We've labeled these groups (in the Introduction) as desired customers, break-even customers, and costly customers. For most firms, the desired customers (usually about 20 percent of all customers) will generate between 150 and 300 percent of total profits; break-even customers (the middle 60 to 70 percent of customers) about break even; and the least profitable, costly customers (10 to 20 percent of all customers), lose 50 to 200 percent of total profits! The "whale curve" in Figure 1.3 demonstrates this range. In short, 80 percent of a typical firm's customers do not provide an acceptable rate of return! Striving to retain them all is suicidal.

In the case of First Chicago, an examination of the profitability of the firm's customers revealed that only 33 percent generated an adequate rate of return (and this is a higher percentage than is typically seen for most firms). Even after changing its policies, that number did not come close to breaking 50 percent, as it topped out at only 44 percent of customers. Clearly, making the majority of customers more loyal is not a wise investment decision for most companies. Instead, managers must make reasoned decisions about which customers truly represent assets to their firms' financial health, and target their loyalty efforts to them.

FIGURE 1.3 Whale Curve

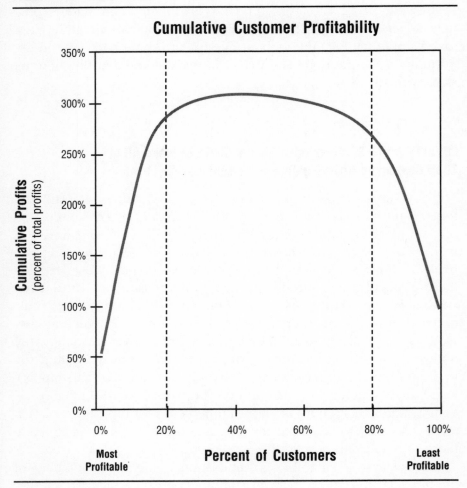

LOYALTY MYTH 4: Companies with More Loyal Customers Will Always Have Higher Market Shares

While it may seem counterintuitive, firms with the highest loyalty levels frequently do not have the highest market shares. Generally, organizations we tend to associate with having fiercely loyal customers represent smaller, exclusive groups: Harley Davidson owners, Fender

Source: Cartoonybin.com. Reproduced with permission.

Stratocaster owners, Jimmy Buffett fans, and so on. The intense loyalty of Macintosh computer users resulted in a *Sociology of Religion* scientific paper entitled "May the Force of the Operating System Be with You: Macintosh Devotion as Implicit Religion." The article described Mac owners' ardent devotion as follows:

> In the case of the Mac enthusiasts, I found deep religious symbolism that is fundamental to the strong devotion to their computer platform. Like a religion, the beliefs of the Mac devotees are founded on the distinction between the sacred and the profane. To many, there is a sacred bond between computers and people—they should work together in harmony, as Mac users often emphasize that Macintosh computers do not "fight back" as other computers do. And, if such a sacred bond between human and computer is maintained, Mac enthusiasts believe that computer technology will help improve humanity. Thus . . . the Macintosh computer, which

symbolizes a spiritual passage to an utopian future, also ties
its followers together. Moreover, the faith of Mac devotees in
this utopian future is expressed through their practices, including their "evangelistic" efforts.[34]

Research regarding customer satisfaction and market share sheds
insight into why there is often a disconnect between loyalty and market share. While satisfaction and loyalty are not the same thing, they
are strongly correlated. The results of various studies on the satisfac-
tion-market share relationship have been mixed, with some finding a
positive relationship while others find a negative relationship.
   There are several reasons proposed for negative relationships. Increases in market share may negatively impact customers' perceptions
of quality both indirectly (for example, decreasing perceived value
due to product overuse) and directly (for example, the loss of exclusivity). A negative correlation can also be a function of the type of
market itself. In relatively homogeneous markets where customer
needs are relatively similar, market share and loyalty will move together. In heterogeneous markets, market share leadership will not
typically be associated with the highest levels of loyalty, as niche play-
ers who address the unique needs of smaller segments will naturally
enjoy a more loyal following—at the expense of being less attractive
to the total market.

LOYALTY MYTH 5: Companies Should Seek to Change Switchers into Loyal Customers

This myth flows from the logic that if customer loyalty drives profitability, then maximizing profits comes from making all customers
loyal (Myth 3). But, as all managers know, different customer types
derive value from their shopping experiences for different reasons.
Two relatively universal customer segments most prone to switching
are customers commonly referred to as *variety seekers* and *deal seekers*. The variety seeker is motivated by curiosity about and the desire
for new experiences in product types and brands. The deal seeker is
primarily motivated by price. Trying to change these customers is like

trying to get a leopard to change its spots—it never works. The customers in these groups are who they are; they are unlikely to change.

The desire to alternate between brands or firms is simply innate in some customers. Despite this truism, firms engage in extensive promotional campaigns, hoping to graduate customers to higher levels of loyalty and profitability. These false hopes have helped to inflate promotional spending to an unbelievable size. The U.S. promotional marketing industry has expanded from $98 billion in 1998 to $233 billion in the year 2002.[35] The impact on companies has been staggering. For example, Kraft allocates approximately 42 cents of every dollar it earns to advertising and promotion. Given this extraordinary expense, one would expect customer loyalty to be at an all-time high. Thirty years ago, Kraft would have classified approximately 40 percent of its customers as loyal. Today, that number is somewhere around 15 percent.[36]

As most consumer package goods companies have discovered, the problem with chasing variety-seeking and deal-seeking customers is that it actually deteriorates customer loyalty across the board. Too many firms have trained their customers to respond to sales promotions by overusing these tactics. Once-loyal customers are actually becoming accustomed to deals and deal days, and are altering their behaviors by putting off scheduled purchases, waiting for deals or promotions.

LOYALTY MYTH 6: Efforts to Improve Customer-Centric Measures Are Properly Separated From Efforts to Improve Brand-Centric Measures

For most firms, marketing has largely focused on brand-centric objectives. Simplistically, brand-centric marketing can be thought of as manipulating the elements of the marketing mix (commonly referred to as the four P's: product, price, promotion, and place) to improve brand equity. In contrast, customer-centric marketing largely focuses on efforts to improve customers' perceptions of their experiences with a firm's products or services, or with the firm itself. In opposition to a brand-centric focus on acquiring more customers (conquest marketing), customer-centricity is aimed largely at retaining customers and developing loyalty with them (retention marketing). Figure 1.4 depicts the differences in these two approaches when it comes to conducting research.

While both brand-centric and customer-centric approaches are aimed at affecting customers' attitudes and behaviors, managers and researchers have tended to dichotomize these functions. Brand management efforts are usually considered separately from satisfaction management efforts in most firms and are frequently the responsibilities of different departments within the organization. Similarly, specialized scholarly journals have evolved for researchers dedicated to the focus of either brand-specific or customer-specific issues. This separation would be fine if customers actually distinguished between the two presentations of the firm. The problem is that brand-centric objectives are important to current customers (for example, reinforcing brand imagery in customers' minds), and customer-

FIGURE 1.4   Customer vs. Market Research

Differences between Customer Research and Marketing Research

	Customer Research	Marketing Research
Purpose	Data collection and communication	Data collection only
How many are included	Census (or as many as reasonably possible)	Sample
View of the population	Population is precious—needs retaining	Population infinite—no concern
How participation is encouraged	Offer opportunity to help improve product/service—high participant involvement	Offer financial incentive—low participant involvement
How information is analyzed	Keep data disaggregated—at the individual level	Aggregated data (e.g., sample averages, proportions, etc.)
Identification of participants	Information is linked to specific individuals, necessary for follow-up	Information collected anonymously
End result	Fix product/service and remedy individual participants' problems	Identify problems
Need for follow-up from survey participation	Requires follow-up—response to issues, questions	No follow-up, considered unethical

Source: Adapted from Douglas R. Pruden and Terry G. Vavra, "Customer Research, Not Marketing Research," *Marketing Research*, 12, No. 2 (Summer 2000), 14–19.

centric objectives are important to attracting new customers (for example, reputation for good customer service and responsiveness to customer needs).

Our own research confirms that brand-centric and customer-centric efforts need to be considered jointly; while each contributes to the share-of-spending (share-of-wallet) a customer allocates to a firm, they also act in a combined fashion.[37] This finding (previously not recognized) indicates that the interaction between the efforts can double the customers' share-of-spending when both are positive or halve it when both are low. This means firms need to find a way to manage both acquisition and retention efforts simultaneously and in a coordinated way if they wish to maximize their profits. This is not easy, as the two perspectives have different origins and different views of the function of marketing. But convergence of these two perspectives is essential, as those firms that do this well will reap substantially greater returns from their customers.

After learning that acquiring customers was far less cost effective than retention, Jacoby, Martin & Company went the extra mile to retain its only remaining customer.

Source: Cartoonybin.com. Reproduced with permission.

LOYALTY MYTH 7: Retaining 5 Percent More of a Company's Customers Will Increase Profits by 25 to 85 Percent

This myth comes directly from what many managers would consider an unimpeachable source: the *Harvard Business Review*. In 1990, Bain & Company consultant Frederick Reichheld and Harvard professor W. Earl Sasser Jr. published a landmark article, "Zero Defections: Quality Comes to Services."[38] The article claims "companies can boost profits by almost 100 percent by retaining just 5 percent more customers." Later in the article it refines the claim to "reducing defections 5 percent boosts profits 25 percent to 85 percent." Without question, this was a seminal article. Almost overnight it validated customer retention and spurred the quest for customer loyalty among firms worldwide. Unfortunately, despite publication in a prestigious journal, the promise is flawed on at least three basic levels.

1. The company needs to be generating relatively small current profit percentages to expect such a high percentage increase (25 to 85 percent). If we assume that there are no additional costs associated with increasing retention rates, and that each customer contributes equally to revenues, a firm would have to have a pathetic 5 percent rate of return in order to increase profits by 100 percent from a five percent increase in retention rates. More typical returns substantially lower the potential financial impact from improved retention, as shown in Figure 1.5.

2. The ability to generate further profits by improving retention is highly contingent upon a firm's current retention rate. If we take away the assumption that there are no additional costs associated with increasing the retention rate for customers, it becomes very likely that there will be diminishing returns. At some point it will no longer be cost effective to dissuade potential defecting customers from defecting. This means that for firms with relatively low retention rates (high churn), it will likely cost less to increase retention by 5 percent than it will for companies with already high customer retention rates. For virtually all firms, it will never be cost effective to retain 100 percent of customers. Therefore, depending upon where a firm is positioned

FIGURE 1.5 Increase from Retention

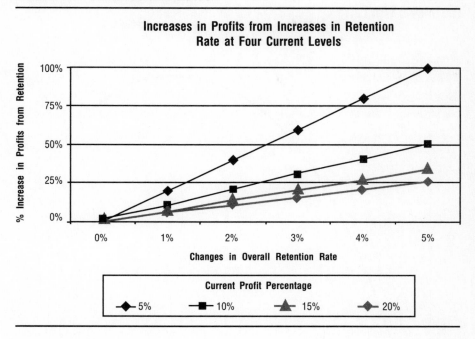

Increases in Profits from Increases in Retention Rate at Four Current Levels

with regard to its retention-profit function, the return on investment of improving customer retention by 5 percent can be either positive or negative. (See Figure 1.6.)

3. For most firms, the most profitable 20 percent of customers generate between 150 and 300 percent of total profits; the middle 60 to 70 percent of customers about break even; and the least profitable 10 to 20 percent of customers lose 50 to 200 percent of total profits. Myth 7's greatest failing is its disregard for how customer profitability is distributed throughout firms' customerbases. For most firms, 20 percent of the customer base (the desired customers) generates the lion's share of the profits, and 10 to 20 percent are significant money losers (costly customers). The size of losses generated by Costly Customers typically determines whether a firm operates in the black or in the red. It doesn't take a rocket scientist to realize that retaining 5 percent more customers won't make money unless they are the *right* customers—those in the top 20 percent.

FIGURE 1.6   Diminishing Returns from Retention

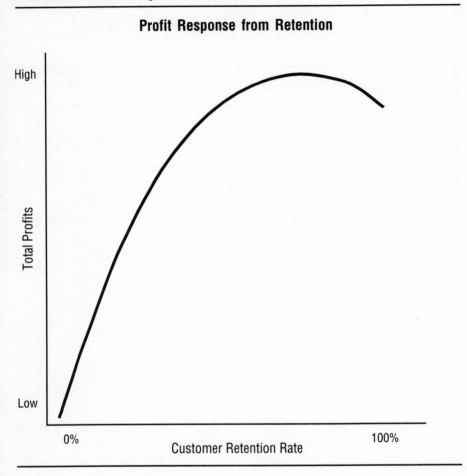

Profit Response from Retention

Total Profits

High

Low

0%   Customer Retention Rate   100%

LOYALTY MYTH 8: It Costs Five Times More to Acquire a New Customer than to Retain a Current Customer

Although it is difficult to determine the exact origins of this platitude, the earliest sources that we can find attribute it to research conducted by the Technical Assistance Research Project (TARP) in Washington, D.C., in the late 1980s.[39] Around the same time, other loyalty pundits claimed exactly the same findings as their own (for example, the Customer Service Institute,[40] Consumer Connections Corp.,[41] and ITEM Group[42]). Soon the myth found its way into the pages of prestigious journals and books. In 1990, Total Quality Management Group president Christopher Hart and Harvard professors James Heskett and W. Earl Sasser, Jr. lent the statement further credibility in their *Harvard Business Review* article "The Profitable Art of Service Recovery."[43] And popular business strategist Tom Peters likewise repeated the myth in his best-selling book *Thriving on Chaos*.[44]

This myth is so pervasive and so seemingly intuitive that it has stood unchallenged for 20 or more years! We, too, have published prior works repeating this fallacy. There is currently enough contrary information to bury or significantly qualify this truism, based on three major flaws.

1. The fundamental financial underpinnings of the argument are either misallocated in terms of acquisition and retention, or the financial effects attributed to retention are false. The basic argument that the cost to acquire new customers is substantially greater than that to retain existing customers hinges on a stream of interrelated factors. With regard to existing customers, there is the assumption that they will (1) increase their level of spending at an increasing rate; (2) purchase at full-margin rather than discount prices; and (3) create operating efficiencies for firms. Unfortunately, none of these things are true, as will be summarily disproved in other parts of this book.

With regard to new customers, operating costs are presumed to rise as the customer has to learn the procedures of the firm, and the firm has to learn the needs of its new customer. Even if that were universally true, most firms don't go through new account setups, credit searches, and so on. when a new customer walks through the door. The fallacy becomes obvious when we think about our own experiences as a new customer. What exactly was the additional cost to the companies of our purchasing from a new retailer, dining at a new restaurant, or flying with a new airline? For those industries in which there is a legitimate cost associated with sign-up, these costs are often incurred regardless of whether the consumer remains loyal to the firm. Exactly how much easier is it to purchase a new car, television, or washing machine simply by staying with the same brand?

The x-factor that makes this myth seem plausible is the costs associated with advertising and promotional expenses. While it is believable that they represent enormous expenses that would far exceed the costs of retaining existing customers, there is one fatal flaw with this assumption: advertising and promotion are not simply about inducing first-time purchases. Much advertising is about reinforcing brand imagery and maintaining awareness among current customers of the brand. And while some firms promotionally "price to lose" to attract new customers in the short term, typically such promotions are enjoyed by both prospective and current customers. Therefore the breakdown of acquisition- versus retention-related expenses associated with advertising and promotion is likely incorrectly weighted to the acquisition side of the equation to arrive at this fallacy.

2. The assertion ignores the life cycle of products, services, and institutions. When firms are in their introductory and growth phases, allocations to acquire customers will be substantial. The customer acquisition-retention cost ratio will typically be heavily weighted to acquisition. Conversely, when products or firms are in the decline phase, allocations required to retain customers will be substantial, making the typical acquisition-retention cost ratio weighted heavily to retention. It is in the maturity phase of a product's life cycle that the ratio of acquisition costs to retention costs can fall to either side.

3. It ignores the fact that a company's customer base is made up of a broad mix of customers who vary in cost to acquire and retain. Managerially, the problem with this myth is that it ignores the heterogeneity of customer bases. The fact is that customers vary dramatically in the costs both to acquire and to retain. As noted earlier, for most firms, customer profitability is not evenly distributed. Any costs associated with retaining customers in the bottom tier, when including their losses to the firm, are likely to far outweigh the costs to the firm of acquiring another customer. Additionally, paying to retain a customer in the large break-even segment is likely to result in the same problem.

Often the most expensive customers to retain are those who generate the most profits for the firm (Desired Customers). For obvious reasons, they are most desirable to competitors, and thus are more likely to receive attractive offers from the competition. Desired Customers also often know that their relationship is significant to the firm and, consequently, expect a higher level of service. The costs to retain these customers can be very high, but economically worthwhile to the firm.

As a result, while it seems plausible that acquisition costs are significantly higher than retention costs, as with all myths, the reality is far more complex. And while it may serve as a provocative wake-up statement to ensure that management is aware of the importance of retaining customers, supporting any retention strategy based in whole upon this myth is a recipe for financial disappointment.

LOYALTY MYTH 9: Companies Should Focus on Their High Share-of-Wallet Customers

The most obvious manifestation of loyalty is customers' consolidation of their related purchases with a single vendor (maximizing their share of requirements with the vendor). In fact, for many product categories, share-of-wallet—not retention—is the most relevant behavioral loyalty metric. For example, Kraft Foods, the largest food and beverage firm in North America, defines a loyal customer as someone who purchases 70 percent or more of the same brand within a category over a three-year-period.[45] Because loyalty and share-of-wallet are inextricably linked, improving wallet share has become an overarching goal of many firms. Unfortunately, like many loyalty myths, its seductiveness belies a complex truth.

As noted earlier, the majority of a firm's customers do not produce an acceptable rate of return, with large percentages actually costing the firm money. In many situations, they are not unprofitable because they have a low share-of-spending with the firm; they are unprofitable because the level of service that they demand exceeds their willingness or ability to pay for goods and services in the category. Efforts to get higher wallet shares across the entire customer base are likely to be an exercise in futility.

Second, customers can have high wallet shares but be totally price driven. For example, a large financial services client found that in one of its product categories, increases in share-of-wallet resulted in correspondingly negative returns.[46] The problem was the price sensitivity of

Source: Cartoonybin.com. Reproduced with permission.

the customer base. Whenever the company offered a lower-priced option, customers quickly snapped up large quantities of the product. Share for these customers was entirely driven by their propensity to seek deals. This, of course, is far from a unique circumstance. Consumer packaged goods firms face this routinely, as they find enormous spikes in their sales related to sales promotions. And while these consumers may be stocking up on their favorite brands, they do so at the manufacturer's expense.

LOYALTY MYTH 10: In Planning for the Future, It's Always Best to Focus on Customers Who Have Contributed the Most to Company Profits

Without question, companies should ensure that their profitable customers are cherished. These customers have demonstrated a commitment by providing the firm with the profits it needs to remain viable.

Therefore, many loyalty-focused organizations choose to focus loyalty efforts on those customers who have generated the most profits to the firm in the past. In terms of a firm's efforts to profit from customer loyalty, however, this practice does not represent the best economic decision.

To pursue this approach, firms typically use a technique called "recency, frequency, and monetary value" (RFM) to detect their best customers. The RFM technique identifies customers who have spent a lot recently and targets them for future marketing activities. The effect is one that we have all experienced. What is the first thing that happens when we give money to most charities or nonprofit organizations? We get flooded with mail asking for more money the next week. This is RFM in action! But it also identifies one of the problems with this approach: Focusing on the volume of past purchasing activity does not necessarily help us understand the underlying purchase patterns. Many purchasing events are one-time or infrequent, but this technique ensures that you will be in the system for quite a while if you have generated significant revenue for the firm. Examining the purchases of a mail order company showed that a large segment of customers made concentrated purchases for a brief period of time, and then never again. Because of the way the RFM scores were calculated, the company kept this group on their active list for 36 months, well after it was profitable to do so. These misguided investments cost this particular company approximately $1 million annually.[47]

Another major problem is that focusing on past profitability ignores life-changing factors that are likely to influence future purchases. Customers get married, are promoted to better-paying jobs, buy homes, have children, and so on, all of which affect their future potential profitability to a company. One large European home products retailer found that by assessing nine key life factors of its customers, it was able to improve the return on investment of its retention expenditures from 2-to-1 to 10-to-1.

LOYALTY MYTH 11: Service Providers Differ Distinctly from Product Manufacturers in How Loyalty Tools Can Be Effectively Applied

Traditionally, people have dichotomized businesses into products and services. If the firm offered a physical product, it fell into the product sector; otherwise, it was classified as a service. This classification schema has had a profound impact on the way managers believe that they can apply tools designed to enhance customer loyalty. With the rise of the quality movement of the 1980s, U.S. and European manufacturers adopted the principles of such noted quality gurus as W. Edwards Deming and J.M. Juran—principles that had already been adopted over a decade earlier by Japanese manufacturers and were touted as the reasons for the success of the Japanese automotive, machine tool, and electronics industries.

The quality tools of Deming and Juran centered on eliminating variation in the manufacturing of products. The problem for service businesses was that the tools that applied to the manufacture of physical products did not work well in service settings (particularly in human interactions). People do not like the feeling that they are being treated like a number. Instead, they want to feel that their issues are being addressed in a manner fitting to their unique circumstances. It is no accident that Reichheld's and Sasser's seminal *Harvard Business Review* paper that propelled the customer loyalty movement was entitled "Zero Defections: Quality Comes to Services." Playing on the common manufacturing quality goal metric of zero defects, Reichheld and Sasser proposed a loyalty metric for services: zero defections (100 percent customer retention). In essence, the customer loyalty movement was established as a parallel quality movement for the service sector.

Because the initial thrust of the loyalty movement was the service sector, it was assumed that manufacturers must have a set of loyalty tools unique from the services sector. Customer loyalty for product companies was believed to focus on the elimination of variation (most frequently noted through what are referred to as Six Sigma programs). Service companies, on the other hand, sought to build customer loyalty through almost the opposite goal—customization of services, maximizing variation. In this way the service delivered to each customer conformed more to his needs than to a general blueprint.

There's just one major flaw with this strict dichotomization. Essentially all goods have a service component, and all services have some form of tangible representation; *there is no such thing as a pure product company.* In essence, everything is a service, though it may or may not have a physical product. While this viewpoint has not yet caught on with the general business community, it is now the accepted viewpoint of the leading service researchers. Christopher Lovelock, the author of the leading textbook on services for the past two decades, and Evert Gummesson observed, "The claim that services are uniquely different from goods [on the characteristics used to define the distinction between product and service companies] is not supported by the evidence."[48]

This may seem like academic minutia, but it is not. In companies traditionally viewed as service-based, efforts to build customer loyalty can be unnecessarily constrained if customization (variation from a standard) is discouraged. The delivery of services must be evaluated slightly differently than conformance of products to a standard. As Robert Eversole, president and CEO of Fifth Third Bank, based in Columbus, Ohio, observed, "In 2003, we had 8.4 billion transactions. We have to be extremely accurate. With that number, even if you are 98 or 99 percent accurate, that leaves a lot of room for error. . . . We printed millions of checking account statements, but if you didn't get yours, you don't care about the millions that did print."[49]

Similarly, companies traditionally viewed as product manufacturers can lose customer loyalty by failing to be customer-focused in the ways they relate to their customers. The U.S. division of Roche Diagnostics, a maker of diagnostic testing equipment, was forced to reengineer its entire phone support structure because it was significantly eroding customer loyalty. As Carlo Medici, former U.S. president of Roche Diagnostics, noted, "[We] ought to 'repair' the customer more than the machine."[50] The tools traditionally associated with enhancing loyalty for manufacturers actually apply to all companies where the determination of delivery quality (the degree to which a firm's offering is reliable, standardized, and free from errors) is driven by customers' expectations. The tools traditionally associated with services apply where customization dictates what customers expect. And because everything is a service, both sets of tools are necessary for all firms.

SETTING THE RECORD STRAIGHT:
LOYALTY AND CORPORATE GOALS

In this chapter we've reviewed eleven myths dealing with customer loyalty subverting organizational goals. Orienting an organization to customer loyalty is a worthy undertaking, and it can be a good long-term strategy for differentiation and survival. But in this chapter we've shown that up to now, it hasn't always been good business. That's because the conventional (mis)understanding of customer loyalty has placed business executives at a distinct disadvantage.

We strongly support customer loyalty as a central mission for organizations so long as there is an adequate understanding of its potential return.

Loyalty Truth 1: Don't manage for customer retention before you manage for customer selection. You probably don't want to keep all of your customers; create and apply loyalty strategies and tactics selectively. Make sure your loyalty efforts are directed primarily to those you wish to keep, and make offers that are relevant to these desired customers.

Companies survive only through profitable operations. Customer loyalty may be a meaningful corporate goal, but only under the proper circumstances and only when directed at a group of customers known to be profitable and therefore desirable to be retained. Blind reliance on loyalty as a universal goal will put you out of business. Any loyalty initiative, therefore, needs to begin with an understanding of the profitability of individual customers. Without such information, retention efforts may be oriented toward and offered to high-cost, low-value customers—an invitation to financial disaster.

Companies who dedicate their operations primarily to customer loyalty (retention marketing) should only do so if their product mix and industry are in the declining phases of the product life cycle. Finally, aiming to convert all customers to loyal customers is a false hope. Customers are who they are. It's far better to accept them as they are and then maintain those with whom a firm can build mutually productive relationships.

U.S. science fiction writer Philip K. Dick understood, "Reality is that which, when you stop believing in it, doesn't go away."[51] As this book has already demonstrated, much of the conventional wisdom about customer loyalty is just plain wrong. Like the most pervasive myths, the logic behind the loyalty myths is seductive, easy to grasp, and appealing to our human desire for fairness. By the end of this book, however, almost everything you've ever heard, read, or seen about customer loyalty will be debunked. The truth about customer loyalty is far more complex than we've been led to believe—but it is no less fair.

CHAPTER 2

Loyalty Myths Contaminating Company Management Practices

Source: Cartoonybin.com. Reproduced with permission.

*You're not in business to be liked. Neither am I. We're here to suc-
ceed. If you want a friend, get a dog. I'm not taking any chances;
I've got two dogs.*[1]

—Albert J. Dunlap, Chairman and CEO, Scott Paper
(April, 1994—December, 1995)

THE PARABLE OF THE PREEMINENT SHAREHOLDER

In 1879, brothers Irvin and Clarence Scott founded Scott Paper in
Philadelphia, Pennsylvania, producing paper bags and wrapping paper.[2] In the 1880s, however, the brothers took a gamble and decided
to enter a virgin market: toilet paper.[3] Although earlier attempts to get
the public to accept the idea of spending money on paper designed
exclusively for use as bathroom tissue had failed, the Scott brothers
had the good fortune to enter the market as the climate was becoming
much more favorable for its product. Indoor plumbing was becoming
more common and major U.S. cities were installing public sewer systems.[4] As America's bathrooms were changing, Americans began to regard toilet tissue as a necessity.

When Scott entered the toilet paper market, it did so quite con-
servatively, selling its toilet paper under private label; but with the
growing acceptance of its product, Scott launched its own brand in
1902: Waldorf.[5] Waldorf ultimately became Scott Tissue—the first successfully marketed toilet paper. Scott's entry into the toilet paper market led to the creation of another incredibly successful product,
Sani-Towels, the first paper towel available in the U.S.[6]

Initially, Scott's Sani-Towels were primarily purchased by hotels,
restaurants, and railroad stations for use in public restrooms. Consumers, on the other hand, were reluctant to spend money for disposable paper towels when the alternative—cloth towels—could be used
repeatedly. Over time, consumers became more appreciative of the
convenience of disposable paper towels. Scott's pioneering efforts resulted in its products becoming a familiar feature in American homes,
and products such as Cottonelle, Viva, and Scotties became household

names.[7] Scott Paper grew to become the world's largest supplier of toilet tissue, paper towels, and paper napkins, with total annual sales exceeding $5 billion,[8] and a truly global organization, with operations in 21 countries and a presence in 59 others.[9]

Lost Bearings

Like many old-style American firms founded toward the end of the Industrial Age, Scott found itself slow to react to changes in the twentieth-century market. As early as the 1960s, tough competition from formidable competitors such as Procter & Gamble began to erode profit margins.[10] By the 1990s, the company found itself seriously off course: It was no longer the leader in most of its major markets and sales were declining, dropping from $5.17 billion in 1990 to $4.75 billion in 1994.[11] With debt increasing to a crushing $2.3 billion, Scott found itself sustaining significant losses, $70 million in 1991 and $277 million in 1993.[12]

In the face of steadily declining earnings, Scott's CEO, Philip Lippincott, initiated three restructurings in four years. Unfortunately, there were no apparent benefits, so in January 1994 Lippincott announced more drastic plans, laying off 25 percent of Scott's work force—8,300 employees—over a three-year period.[13] Lippincott never saw his plan implemented. He announced his retirement from the company where he had spent his entire career and 12 years as CEO.[14]

New Captain

Concluding that the company needed a revolutionary change in direction, Scott's board of directors selected a CEO from outside the company (a first in the company's 115-year history).[15] Albert J. Dunlap, a West Point graduate and former paratrooper, had a history of restructuring troubled companies. Dunlap was referred to as "Chainsaw Dunlap" or "Rambo in Pinstripes" by his many critics, although the nicknames were given to him as compliments by two of his admirers. To lure him from retirement, the board offered him a $1 million per year five-year contract and gave him a mandate to transform Scott Paper.[16] Dunlap's modus operandi was to cut sharply and rapidly. When Dunlap took the helm of a company, it usually meant that he would divest it of businesses he believed to be outside of the core business, fiercely attack costs, and initiate massive layoffs. His stated philosophy on restructuring a company was "do it once, do it severely, and get it over with."[17]

Immediately after taking over as CEO in April 1994, Dunlap changed Scott's course. To quote Dunlap:

> My honeymoon with Scott lasted only as long as it took the elevator to reach the sixth floor. I ordered members of the company's 11-member ruling management committee immediately into a meeting. "Ladies and gentlemen," I said, "this could be the best day of your life or it could be the worst." By my reputation alone, they knew what I meant. For those who hadn't performed—virtually all of them—it would be the worst day of their professional lives. Days went by in a rush of meetings, ultimatums, firings. In due course, the 11-member operating committee was disbanded. Two of its members were given increased responsibilities. The others resigned, were reassigned, or were fired."[18]

Dunlap greatly admired a kill-or-be-killed type of self-sufficiency. In his office at Scott, two brass ornaments depicting circling sharks were prominently displayed.[19] "I respect predators because they live off their wits," he said. "No one is bringing their meals to the table. No one is taking care of them. No one is providing anything for them; they have to provide for themselves. The independence of predators—that I respect."[20]

That viewpoint appears to hold for his opinions of humans as well. For example, while touring one of Scott's plants, an employee proudly told Dunlap that he was a 30-year veteran. Dunlap's loyalty-critical reply: "Why would you stay with a company for 30 years?"[21] With Dunlap now in charge, many Scott employees would find long-term employment was no longer an option. In creating his reorganization plan for Scott, Dunlap quickly determined that (1) the layoffs proposed by his predecessor were too small and occurred over too long a period;[22] (2) many of Scott's assets should be sold; and (3) costs needed to be aggressively cut, including paring down many of Scott's product offerings and slashing spending on research and development and staff training.[23]

New Loyalties

All of Dunlap's restructuring efforts were designed for one purpose only: to focus exclusively on shareholders. Dunlap held the belief that the concept of corporate stakeholders (employees, communities, etc.) was "total rubbish" and had little tolerance for managers who allowed stakeholder concerns to affect their decisions.[24] "I looked at the managers," said Dunlap. "I listened to them talking about their priorities, their constituencies. I heard somebody talk about constituencies like the community, like employees—I think he went through *six* constituencies. 'Wait a minute,' I said. 'You have only *one* constituency: (our) shareholders.'"[25] Under Dunlap, undivided loyalty to the shareholder was more than rhetoric—it was obligatory. Scott went so far as to forbid managers to be involved in community activities since it would take away from business activities.[26] Furthermore, the company canceled its charitable contributions and abolished Scott's charitable foundation.[27]

Although Dunlap talked of remaking Scott into a world-class consumer products company, it is clear that he was considering selling the company within months of becoming CEO; Salomon Brothers Inc. had been retained in late 1994 to begin shopping the company to prospective buyers.[28] Dunlap made his desire to sell clear to shareholders as early as April 1995, just one year after becoming CEO, telling them, "Everything but your family and your dogs in this world is for sale at the right price."[29] A buyer for Scott was found. On December 12, 1995, Scott's shareholders approved a merger with Kimberly-Clark Corporation valued at $9.4 billion, creating a $12 billion global consumer products company. Kimberly-Clark agreed to pay Dunlap $20 million in an extraordinarily lucrative non-compete agreement, and, all told, he pocketed nearly $100 million for his 603 days of work at Scott, about $50 million of which was from stock options.[30]

Dunlap boasted: "The Scott story will go down in the annals of American business history as one of the most successful, quickest turnarounds ever."[31] He definitely transformed Scott Paper. The effect was impressive. Under Dunlap, Scott's stock price went from $38 per share to $112 in 18 months.[32] As a result, he increased the value of the company by $6.3 billion and, because of his aggressive cost cutting and price increases, Scott reached record earnings during Dunlap's last quarter as CEO.[33] Such results garnered him supporters; in a survey of CEOs by *Financial World* magazine in 1995, Dunlap was named as one of the most admired CEOs in the U.S.[34]

The Moral of the Preeminent Shareholder

The story of Scott Paper and Al "Chainsaw" Dunlap represents an extreme case of management perspectives being completely disconnected from customer loyalty, yet being extremely successful financially. It points to one unmistakable fact: Companies do not have to manage for customer loyalty to substantially improve their financial performance. Most business schools today teach that the surest path to long-term survival is by satisfying customer needs and wants at a profit. In essence, the goal of business has been redefined as enhancing customer loyalty. So we would expect the operational structures of companies to be oriented to accomplishing this goal. This recent ded-

Franz misunderstood the concept of riding the bull market.

Source: Cartoonybin.com. Reproduced with permission.

ication to customer loyalty has fostered numerous truisms impacting the management perspectives of most companies worldwide. The unfortunate reality is that they are almost all untrue. Their failure to universally apply is the reason Al Dunlap could walk away with $100 million for less than two years' worth of work practicing the antithesis of customer loyalty-oriented management.

Following are some of the most pervasive myths regarding current management perspectives as they pertain to customer loyalty. The first myth is an unalterable consequence of developed economies that simply must be acknowledged and confronted. The remaining myths pertain to the natural structure of organizations that can and must be fixed if firms are to profitably compete through improved customer loyalty.

LOYALTY MYTH 12: Shareholders Manage for Loyalty; the Market Rewards Customer Loyalty

Warren Buffett is widely regarded as one of the greatest investors in history, having amassed a staggering $36 billion fortune largely on his uncanny ability to pick the right stocks. His company, Berkshire Hathaway, only employs 13 people full-time, yet it generates billions of dollars in profits and consistently ranks in the top 10 of *Fortune* magazine's "Most Admired" companies. To explain the company's investment philosophy, Buffett issued an *Owner's Manual* for its stockholders, in which he outlined his general investment principles:

> You should be fully aware of one attitude Charlie [Charles Munger, Buffett's partner and vice chairman] and I share that hurts our financial performance: Regardless of price, we have no interest at all in selling any good businesses that Berkshire owns. We are also very reluctant to sell sub-par businesses as long as we expect them to generate at least some cash and as long as we feel good about their managers and labor relations. . . . Nevertheless, gin rummy managerial behavior (discard your least promising business at each turn) is not our style. We would rather have our overall results penalized a bit than engage in that kind of

behavior. . . . At Berkshire, you will find no "big bath" accounting maneuvers or restructurings nor any "smoothing"
of quarterly or annual results. . . . Most of our managers are
independently wealthy, and it's therefore up to us to create
a climate that encourages them to choose working with
Berkshire over golfing or fishing. This leaves us needing to
treat them fairly and in the manner that we would wish to
be treated if our positions were reversed.[35]

Berkshire Hathaway's results have been nothing short of outstanding, beating the average return of the S&P 500 in 30 of the past
31 years. Clearly Berkshire Hathaway represents the paragon of loyalty investors, buying companies that they recognize as delivering real
value for their customers, and relying on the management of these
companies in good times and in bad. Given Buffett's tremendous success and simple philosophy, it would appear logical that every firm
could expect no less from its shareholders. But we all know that Buffett's tremendous success is the exception rather than the rule. The
more appropriate observation with regard to investor loyalty is, "You
are only as popular as your last earnings statement."

Research shows that CEO compensation and workforce reduc-
tions are highly correlated. Firms that announce layoffs pay their
CEOs more and give them higher raises than firms without at least
one layoff announcement in the previous year, and layoffs tend to be
associated with higher stock prices.[36] The reason is simple: A firm
may be owned by thousands of shareholders but, for most companies, fewer than 100 investors really matter.[37] Most are large institutional investors that have short-term profit objectives driving their
investment decisions. These investors look for short-term performance, not long-term sustainability.

Compounding this short-sightedness are the methods of stock analysts. In their assessment of a company's fundamentals, they almost
never consider customer satisfaction and loyalty information in their
projections for the company's future performance. For example, Tom
Goetzinger, a noted Morningstar Inc. analyst, assigns little importance
to customer satisfaction levels.[38] The authors' own research of portfolio managers finds that Goetzinger is far from alone. Studies have

demonstrated that firms with higher customer loyalty *ultimately* perform better in the marketplace, but winning through customer loyalty takes time, and the 100 investors that really matter have little patience for long-run results.

LOYALTY MYTH 13: Most Companies Are Structured to Build Customer Loyalty

Perhaps the only truly significant organizational structure innovation of the modern era was that of Alfred P. Sloan Jr., the innovative leader of General Motors (GM) for more than 30 years. He championed the decentralization of the company into divisional operating units, placing an executive in charge of each division with authority for its operation. The divisions were guided by a degree of central control. In particular, central management undertook the development of corporate strategy. Without question, Sloan was a visionary, and his success in turning GM into the largest corporation in the world is the stuff of legends.

The Sloan method is no longer revered by management gurus. Chief among their concerns is that it is focused not on the customer but on business processes. The argument came into vogue that a perfect post-Sloan company would be almost structureless, glued together by corporate culture and a focus on customers. Thus evolved (in the mid-1990s) a new organizational structure called *horizontalism*, which claimed to put the customer at the center of the organization. Both *Business Week* and *Fortune* magazines prominently featured stories on the rise of the new management paradigm of the twenty-first century.[39] *Fortune* magazine described the difference between the Sloan system and the horizontal corporation this way:

> Rather than focusing single-mindedly on financial objectives or functional goals, the horizontal organization emphasizes customer satisfaction. Work is simplified and hierarchy flattened by combining related tasks—for example, an account-management process that subsumes the sales, billing, and service functions—and eliminating work that does not add

value. Information zips along an internal superhighway: The knowledge worker analyzes it, and technology moves it quickly across the corporation instead of up and down, speeding up and improving decision-making.[40]

Business Week noted that organizational charts are starting to look strange, describing one company's as looking like a pizza, with each pepperoni representing a cross-functional team. The article listed six companies that used or were moving toward the horizontal model: Lexmark International, General Electric, AT&T, Eastman Chemical, Motorola, and Xerox.

Anyone who had followed the performance of these six firms since the mid-1990s would point out that there have been some very sour moments for at least four of the six: AT&T has posted billions of dollars in losses and has been acquired; Eastman Chemical and Motorola have racked up significant losses and been forced to restructure; Xerox found itself billions in debt, losing market share, cutting its workforce by one-third, and in an accounting scandal, where it was forced to pay $10 million to settle with the Securities and Exchange Commission. Given success stories like these, it's apparent why it is next to impossible to find an article within the past five years that discusses horizontalism, much less extols it as the wave of the future. It appears that the only firms practicing horizontalism are either asleep or dead.

Despite the multitude of management buzzwords and organizational theories that have arisen in the modern era, the structure of virtually every business still bears a strong resemblance to those of the early Industrial Revolution. The model is the military, where there is a clear chain of command. As a *Business Week* editorial noted, "Information flowed up from the bottom, and orders flowed down from the top. Generations of managers could point to pyramid-shaped organizational charts and tell you exactly where they stood. Given the 100 years of phenomenal success that the hierarchical corporate model has had, real change is far easier to talk about than to implement."[41] Apparently, the hierarchical model still rules, but the problems of lack of customer focus remain.

Source: Cartoonybin.com. Reproduced with permission.

LOYALTY MYTH 14: Companies Tend to Know Their Customers

Perhaps the most common statement we hear when starting work with a new client is, "We know our customers, what they want, and what we need to improve." This, of course, is rarely based on anything scientific. Rather, it comes from the gut-level feeling of managers who live their businesses. The problem is, despite the many firms we have worked with over the years, after speaking with their customers, we have never found this to be the case!

The idea that companies tend to know their customers is a myth. We know this from our own experiences as customers. How many companies really know anything about us? A classic IBM commercial features customers in a focus group facility screaming, "You don't know me" at company representatives behind the one-way mirror. Even if some people in the organization know the customers, this

Are you certain that you are a customer of ours, Mr. Jacoby? I am unable to find your information in my Rolo... customer database.

Source: Cartoonybin.com. Reproduced with permission.

knowledge may not be shared, as other agendas may mitigate the desire to share.

The fact is, most companies do not actively engage their customers in a dialogue. Whereas many try to gauge their customers' levels of satisfaction, most do it only as a "temperature check." They do not want to get too much feedback because they lack the internal mechanisms for dealing with it. This is shortsighted. A large-scale study published in the *Journal of Consumer Research* found that clients who were surveyed were more likely to have increased business, half as likely to have defected, and more profitable than clients who were not surveyed.[42] The study noted that these results held for up to 12 months after the survey.

LOYALTY MYTH 15: Most Companies' Databases Are Adequate for Building Loyalty

Most companies keep terrible records of their customers. Some of the largest firms in the world do not even have a database with the key contact information for their largest customers. The information frequently rests in the minds, drawers, or—if they are lucky—computers of their internal sales representatives. It only takes the receipt of a few irrelevant offers for products we could not possibly want for us to recognize that, for all the talk of the computer revolution, it hasn't made its way into our relationships with the companies from which we buy.

The problem is that it is more difficult than promised. In commenting on the results of a 2004 survey of business technology professionals, *Information Week* magazine concluded:

> A 360-degree view of the customer is so tantalizing that most companies are virtually drooling over the prospect of being able to sell, service, market, cross-sell, and up-sell from a common view of a customer's history. The problem is how to get there. As simple as the idea sounds, achieving a complete customer view has proved as elusive as the search for the Holy Grail. The holdup: integration. Business-technology professionals say the greatest issue in customer-information management is the variety of data sources from which they must pull information.[43]

There are a few rare, well-publicized examples of companies with well-equipped databases:

- Harrah's Entertainment. Its systems can predict a customer's spending behavior and how long they will stay by a customer's third visit. As a result, Harrah's can target customers for specific promotions and provide real-time incentives.[44]
- USAA (the financial services company that serves the US military). The systems of the different USAA companies are integrated and designed so that they anticipate customer needs that USAA can help satisfy. For example, when a customer calls about purchasing an automobile, a USAA representative can arrange the financing, arrange the insurance, set up a bank account to automatically deduct car and insurance payments, and even order an infant car seat.[45]

Source: Cartoonybin.com. Reproduced with permission.

Unfortunately, Harrah's and USAA are the exception, which is why our mailboxes remain full of letters beginning "Dear Valued Customer."

LOYALTY MYTH 16: Companies Are Generally Willing to Address the Needs of Individual Customers

Despite all the talk of one-to-one marketing and customer-centric organizations, most companies are volume-driven entities that struggle with variation. Handling individual customer needs typically requires that actions deviate from the standard processes, which means that more employees will have to be involved to customize the solution. This is the antithesis of their business model. Firms want happy customers and they want to meet their needs, but most want customers to be happy and fulfilled with the products and services that they have offered to the market, as is.

Most of us have answered a questionnaire or sent in a comment

Source: Cartoonybin.com. Reproduced with permission.

card; most of us have had the experience of getting absolutely no feedback; and virtually none of us have heard follow-up as to how, if at all, the firm has changed its processes to address our concerns or recommendations. Even registering a formal complaint has a good chance of being ignored. Research shows that over 20 percent of written complaints will not get a response.[46] The ultimate promise of a customer loyalty strategy is that firms will sell the right product, at the right price, at the right time, to the right customer. That may very well be the future, but for most firms, it is not the present.

LOYALTY MYTH 17: Companies with Continuous Customer Relationships Have an Advantage in Building Loyalty over Other Companies

This myth flows from two observed facts about customer loyalty: (1) Loyal customers typically purchase more frequently from a company;

and (2) the length of time between initial purchase and repurchase tends to negatively influence repurchase of the same brand. If loyal customers tend to have contact with the company more frequently, and long repurchase cycles negatively affect loyalty, then one could reasonably conclude that those firms with continuous relationships have the advantage in terms of building customer loyalty.

Unfortunately, it does not work like that. Most companies that have continuous relationships with customers are in low-involvement services (insurance, retail banking, utilities, etc.). While customers may expend considerable effort in the initial search, interaction is typically infrequent despite the continuity of the relationship. Customers tend not to think about these services except when there is a problem. If these firms have any advantage, it is that there is typically a cost to switch (for example, switching banks can mean reconciling outstanding checks, and switching life insurance carriers will mean new medical exams and paperwork). Although these switching costs can make

Source: Cartoonybin.com. Reproduced with permission.

customers stick with a provider, holding customers hostage is not what is meant by loyalty.

Even if we assume that continuous relationships extend to the purchase of automobiles and large consumer durables, an examination of repurchase data shows that ownership does not equate to repeat purchase. The best automobile repurchase rate is under 70 percent, and most fall well under 50 percent—hardly an endorsement of ownership experience. Furthermore, long-term, continuous relationships have the potential of growing stale in customers' minds.[47] This is easy to understand—a trip to an amusement park can be exciting, but if you went every day, it would begin to appear ordinary. The adage "Absence makes the heart grow fonder" may very well apply for some firms with regard to loyalty.

SETTING THE RECORD STRAIGHT:
LOYALTY AND MANAGEMENT PRACTICES

Regardless of the sincerity of managers' desires to improve customer loyalty, most firms lack the structure, systems, processes, and right-minded owners to successfully make the journey. Despite all the money that companies have sunk into information technology (IT), the systems are only as good as the data they hold. Even if the IT systems were pristine, it does little good to have high-quality customer information if the structures of companies thwart its effective use.

Loyalty Truth 2: Customer loyalty takes more time to grow than most management teams have to give; planning and patience are required.

The truth is executive lifetimes are frequently shorter than the lifetimes of the customers they are trying to retain. If a CEO can't show an increased bottom line, she may be looking for a new job tomorrow. And corporate boards and shareholders can be even less patient.

Databases are currently the vogue, but few companies have the correct information from which to launch a proper loyalty program. The foundation of any good loyalty initiative is information.

The failure of the horizontal corporation to succeed (or even to catch on) demonstrates that building a flatter organization with customers as a central focus is no small task. Nonetheless, the vast majority of managers must begin to recognize that the emperor literally has no clothes. Despite their assertions to the contrary, their firms are unprepared to effectively implement customer loyalty strategies.

CHAPTER 3

Loyalty Myths about Customers: Their Needs, Behaviors, and Referrals

Source: Cartoonybin.com. Reproduced with permission.

We don't fall over ourselves if they say, "My granny fell ill." What part of no refund don't you understand? You are not getting a re-fund so fuck off.[1]

—Michael O'Leary, CEO, Ryanair

Deregulation has transformed the airline industry for much of the world. In the United States, it has resulted in the rise of low-fare, point-to-point carriers. The most heralded of these carriers has been Southwest Airlines. Its success has been attributed to an almost folkloric mixture of clever business strategy with a unique, people-friendly corporate culture. In fact, five highly respected Harvard professors argued in the *Harvard Business Review* that Southwest was a penultimate example of the "Service-Profit Chain."[2] Simply put, Southwest was successful because of a cycle of good service, from employees to customers—building loyalty among both constituencies and thereby driving profitability.

Perhaps the service-profit chain actually does explain the success of Southwest. In contrast, another airline that has grown tremendously during the 1990s claims to have patterned itself after the Southwest model—but it seems relatively certain that this airline's growth is the result of anything but a "cycle of good service."

THE PARABLE OF EFFICIENCY OVER SERVICE

As in the United States, the 1997 deregulation of the European airline industry under the EU's "Open Skies" policy has resulted in a dramatic change in fortunes for carriers.[3] State carriers, which once had a stranglehold on routes, now find themselves competing with low-cost, no-frills airlines.

The most aggressive and arguably the most successful of these airlines has been an upstart from Ireland, Ryanair. The airline was founded in 1985 by the Ryan family. Their goal: to break the duopoly of British Airways and Aer Lingus on the London-Dublin route. By 1990, however, their defiant enterprise had a loss of 20 million pounds sterling. So in 1991 the family called in Michael O'Leary, then a financial adviser to the company, to rescue the firm. He was made deputy CEO at the age of 29.[4]

To help with his turnaround mission, O'Leary went on a pilgrimage to Southwest Airlines in Dallas. As the result of a meeting with Herbert Kelleher, the guru of Southwest Airlines, O'Leary hit upon a new vision for Ryanair. He decided to switch the airline's business model to mimic that of Southwest: low fares, quick turnarounds of aircraft, high load factors, new jets, and reliance on secondary airports.[5] "It was one of these road-to-Damascus things," notes O'Leary. "We saw Kelleher and his crew do it—and we said, 'Why can't we do this in Europe?' "[6]

What Ryanair did not mimic, however, was Southwest Airlines's culture. Herb Kelleher, co-founder of Southwest Airlines, established a positive relationship between management and union workers, believing the quality of this relationship to be fundamental to the airline's success. Some would go so far as to suggest that Kelleher actually encouraged union membership.[7] O'Leary, however, took a very different approach. He was known for berating employees when they contemplated joining a union. Ryanair suffered a public relations fiasco as the result of its handling of a strike by its baggage handlers in Dublin.[8]

As for its treatment of customers, Ryanair is a low-frills airline in every sense of the word. If you want a drink, a snack, or even a wheelchair to take you to the gate, you must pay for it. (The airline's less than helpful assistance for the disabled likewise resulted in another public relations disaster, with newspapers dedicating columns to the grievances of handicapped Ryanair customers.) There are no blankets or pillows, no frequent flier miles, and no refunds, and airsickness bags are only distributed by request.[9] In explaining the airline's fee-for-everything policy, O'Leary retorted, "No, we shouldn't give you a bloody cup of coffee. We only charge 19 euros for a ticket."[10]

As a result of this posturing, Ryanair has received a less than stellar reputation for customer relations. Notes the *Washington Post*, "Ryanair is not every consumer's cup of tea. While airline officials boast of its on-time record and efficiency, the company has a reputation for handling customer complaints in a manner that ranges from brusque to downright rude."[11] laments Jeff Randall of London's *Sunday Telegraph*:

> During the past four years, I've been predicting that Ryanair's extraordinary journey from obscurity to Europe's Number 1 no-frills operator would end in tears. Hitherto, I've been completely wrong. But I simply refuse to accept that a company with such a cavalier disregard for customer relations can sustain market leadership in a service industry. . . . O'Leary's business philosophy is simple: Ryanair charges the lowest fares, so passengers have no grounds for complaint when the plane is late or bags are lost (which they often are). For a tenner there and back, what do the punters expect? His like-it or lump-it approach is brutal. . . . My own experiences of Ryanair showed an airline that was nothing if not consistent: consistently awful. . . . There are only so many insults even the most price-sensitive customers will take. For long-term success, a brand needs to be loved, not resented."[12]

The Moral of Efficiency over Service

The end result of O'Leary's strategy has ironically been rapid growth and sustained high profits. Notes O'Leary, "In head-to-head competition, low prices will always beat out 'value services.' "[13] Whether Ryanair can remain a high flier is unclear. But what is clear is that O'Leary, in an industry noted for seeking to create customer loyalty through customer service, has been able to differentiate his operation with a low cost, "take it or leave it" approach. It is ironic that, in the industry that established the first highly desired loyalty program, one of the most profitable airlines in the early part of the 2000s would be an airline with a CEO who unapologetically says to customers, "You paid us a fare of €19 —go away."[14]

As Ryanair clearly demonstrates, customer loyalty is not a necessary condition for profitability. Most other airlines probably have higher percentages of truly loyal customers than does Ryanair. Yet, the airline has grown in an era which has seen many industry leaders go bankrupt—unmistakably demonstrating that there are a number of myths about customer loyalty and its impact on customers' spending patterns that don't always find their way to a company's bottom line.

LOYALTY MYTH 18: Most Customers Want to Be Loyal— Customers Want a Relationship with the Firms with Which They Do Business

"Most customers want a relationship," proclaims Mike Gould, chairman and chief executive of Bloomingdale's.[15] Most managers would wholeheartedly accept that as gospel, for two reasons. First of all, most managers eat, sleep, and live their firms' offerings, so they are as biased as are parents of newborns on the beauty and intelligence of their children. While they realistically don't expect customers to be equally zealous toward their firms' products, like proud parents, they do tend to overestimate the importance of their company or brand to their customers.

Second, managers desperately want relationships with their customers because they believe relationships will secure the future of their businesses. And while this, too, is a false assumption, an important mitigating factor is the cachet their brand or company may offer. Is a department store truly a relevant component of one's life? Probably not. And yet blasé New Yorkers have for many years flaunted parcels from Bloomingdale's, in the store's well-recognized "big brown bag."

A fundamental tenet of the customer loyalty movement is the belief that most customers actually want a relationship with the firms with which they conduct business. And while the Bloomingdale's example provides an exception, the concept of the universality of this motive hangs on two false premises:

1. The idea that this tenet applies to "most customers."

2. The belief that it generalizes to all firms.

A walk down any grocery store aisle raises one immediate objection to this idea. The Food Marketing Institute estimates that the average suburban grocery store has in excess of 30,000 SKUs (stock keeping units—i.e., products).[16] The sheer number of product categories from which consumers purchase today makes establishing relationships with even a few companies an arduous task.

Even more compelling is the notion of involvement. With how many of these product categories can a consumer actually feel a strong sense of involvement? Consumers, as we've previously documented, strive for simplicity in their lives. Creating relationships with manufacturers of products in low-involvement categories is not a way to simplify one's life.

That's why relationship approaches don't work particularly well with low-risk, low-involvement items, or when customers buy products on impulse, or when a purchase is triggered by the need to experience variety. And these motives account for a substantial percentage of daily purchases.

Source: Cartoonybin.com. Reproduced with permission.

The reality is that for some categories and businesses, customers *do* wish to create a relationship with the firm or brand, particularly where there is some importance associated with the decision or for brands that offer considerable cachet (e.g., Bloomingdale's). But for a large proportion of purchases, especially those in the business-to-business (B2B) world, consumers primarily want a brand to reduce the costs of their purchase (e.g., in time, risk, and relationship). That doesn't mean a company can't develop a loyal customer base if it is in certain product categories, but it does mean that the intensity of the relationship will largely be dictated by its product category.

LOYALTY MYTH 19: It Is in the Customer's Interest to Have Monogamous Relationships with Companies

Customer loyalty pundits talk of loyalty as an exclusive, one-to-one bond between a customer and a company with emotions reminiscent of a Celine Dion love song. There is, however, a problem with this romantic depiction. While customers may have formed relationships with some companies or brands that exclude competitors, these relationships typically do not exclude *all* competitors.

Researchers Ehrenberg and Goodhardt examined purchase data gathered over a 20-year period in Britain, continental Europe, Japan, and the United States, covering a wide variety of product categories.[17] What they found was that for the most frequently purchased consumer goods, only around 10 percent of customers were completely loyal to a solitary brand, and even in services, exclusive loyalty represented a small percentage of buyers as well. Worse still, monogamously loyal customers typically were light buyers of the products or services! ("Light buyers" are those who purchase far less than the average volume of a product or service. As such, they account for very little revenue.)

It appears that predicting customer loyalty is closer to quantum physics than it is to matrimony. As in quantum physics, probabilities dictate the likelihood that a particular outcome will be observed. Customer loyalty can be thought of as a propensity to buy a particular brand, with the most probable purchase representing the brand with the greatest level of customer loyalty.

Researchers Dowling and Uncles observe:[18]

> "Polygamous loyalty" better describes actual consumer behavior than either brand switching (a conscious once-and-for-all change of allegiance to another brand, as if propensities were 100 percent or zero) or promiscuity (the butterfly tendency to flit from brand to brand without any fixed allegiance, when there are no long-run propensities, only next-purchase probabilities). Polygamous loyalty is readily apparent, for instance, in the soft drink and breakfast cereal markets but extends well beyond to car rentals, fast-food outlets, and business airline travel. It is also evident in customers' memberships in multiple loyalty schemes. For example, surveys of European business airline travelers show that more than eighty percent are members of more than one airline loyalty scheme.

Many of the reasons for polygamous loyalty are straightforward. Consumers switch brands for a particular purchase when:

- The preferred brand is out of stock.
- A competing brand offers better value because of a special promotion.
- Different occasions dictate the need for products of differing levels of quality.
- Variety or novelty is desired.

Given these varying circumstances, a monogamous commitment would prevent consumers from capitalizing on or responding to any or all of these factors. As a result, frequently when customers switch brands they are not rejecting their current brand, ending their loyalty, nor are they lost forever—they are simply acting in their present best interests.

Source: Cartoonybin.com. Reproduced with permission.

LOYALTY MYTH 20: Repeat Purchase Equals Loyalty

Without question, loyalty matters to managers because it affects customers' purchasing behaviors. While they would also appreciate customers referring their product or business to other potential customers, for most companies the primary benefit of customer loyalty is the repeat purchases they can be expected to make.

One of the mistakes that managers and researchers most frequently make, however, is confusing necessity with loyalty. For example, travelers may repeatedly use an airline they dislike simply because the airline offers the only nonstop route to their destination. They look and act loyal, but they're not thinking loyal. Were an alternative carrier available, they would immediately switch. Too often hostaged customers are read as loyal customers.

But even when necessity isn't the reason for repeat purchase, it would be incorrect to presume that repeat purchase equals loyalty. As noted in the prior myth, customers tend to engage in polygamous loyalty. Therefore loyalty can in part be thought of as the probability a customer will purchase a brand on any particular purchase occasion. For example, a customer may tend to purchase Brand A 70 percent of the time, Brand B 20 percent, and Brand C 10 percent of the time. Brand C may consider the customer loyal because he purchased Brand C for his last two purchases, but these purchases could actually reflect the most preferred brand being out of stock, or the result of Brand C being offered at an exceptionally low price.

LOYALTY MYTH 21: A Dissatisfied Customer Will Never Conduct Business with an Offending Firm Again

This myth has at its origins a seminal study conducted for the U.S. government's White House Office of Consumer Affairs, which explicitly stated that "91% of dissatisfied customers will never buy from (an) offending company again."[19] This statement, however, is like an old joke about childbirth: If men and women had to alternate who had the baby, then no family would have more than three children (i.e., men would never undergo childbirth for a second time).

The fact is that time really does heal most wounds, and our vehemence about past perceived injustices tends to fade with time. Virtually all of us have found ourselves purchasing from firms that have dissatisfied us in the past, even if we had sworn that we would never set foot in the establishment again. One of the most endearing qualities in all of us is our capacity to forgive and forget.

Our own purchasing behavior reflects this fact. While we may penalize companies that have dissatisfied us in the past (with reduced purchase frequency, or even outright discontinued shopping for an extended period of time), for the most part we let the infractions go unless they are so egregious that we deem them worthy of time in prison. Researchers Rust, Lemon, and Zeithaml noted that managers and academics alike have frequently treated defecting customers as lost for good. They argued that a more realistic scenario is that cus-

Source: Cartoonybin.com. Reproduced with permission.

tomers may leave and return, and be either serially monogamous or polygamous in terms of the number of firms with which they conduct business in a given category.[20]

LOYALTY MYTH 22: Once a Loyal Customer, Always a Loyal Customer

Most of us know intellectually that this is a myth, but you would not know it from the way loyalty pundits describe loyal customers. Loyal customers tend to be described in language usually reserved for patriots or saints. We are not joking. Take, for example, the following description from Harvard professors Jones and Sasser, published in the *Harvard Business Review.*

> The loyalist is a customer who is completely satisfied and keeps returning to the company. The loyalist is a company's bedrock. This customer's needs and the company's product

or service offerings fit exceptionally well, which, not surprisingly, is why loyalists often are the easiest customers to
serve. . . . Within the loyalist camp are individuals who are
so satisfied, whose experience so far exceeds their expectations, that they share their strong feelings with others. They
are apostles.[21]

Therefore, by inference, based upon the language used, a lost
"loyalist" would be considered a "traitor," and a lost "apostle" a
"heretic." Indeed, even the terms *terrorist* and *saboteur* frequently
turn up in books on loyalty. This is an extreme extrapolation for a
mere business association. And while the language used for customer loyalty doesn't literally state "once loyal, always loyal," it does
carry the ethos of the U.S. Marines Corps motto, "Semper fidelis"
("always faithful").

Unfortunately for most managers, the vast majority of their loyal
customers would not classify themselves as apostles for a company.
And, even more unfortunate, while loyal customers are more likely to
remain with a firm, once-loyal, lost-customers rarely view themselves
as traitors when they switch firms although they may indeed view the
firm they've abandoned as having betrayed them.

A simple examination of the shifts in fortunes of various firms or
brands demonstrates that customer loyalty is indeed a fickle commod-
ity. For example, a study of 353 brands in 21 categories over five years
found that about one-third of the brands experienced market share
changes (increases or decreases) of at least 50 percent. About half of
all smaller brands gained or lost at least 50 percent of their starting
market share, and the same applied to about 20 percent of larger
brands.[22] These findings clearly demonstrate that customer loyalty, unlike loyalty from a pet, must be consistently earned.

LOYALTY MYTH 23: Loyalty Declines as More Purchases Are Made

The origin of this myth lies in observed consumer purchase patterns.
In particular, researchers have found that as goods within a category
are purchased with higher frequencies, the share any particular brand

gets declines. For example, consumers who purchase the product only once have clearly given 100 percent of their share of spending to a single brand. As the number of purchases in the category increases, there is a greater probability that customers will try alternatives, thereby lowering the average share for any one brand. This is illustrated by the graph in Figure 3.1.

Without question, this is a statistical fact. More purchases by a customer reduce the share-of-spending allocated to a particular brand on average. But does that mean that customers become emotionally less loyal?

The first thing to note about the decline in share-of-spending is that it is not linear. In Figure 3.1, as purchase frequency increases from 5 to 15, there is a sharp decline in share; a more moderate decline occurs as purchases increase from around 16 to 60; and there is almost no decline when purchases exceed 60. Researchers Stern and Hammond observed,

FIGURE 3.1   Share of Category Purchases

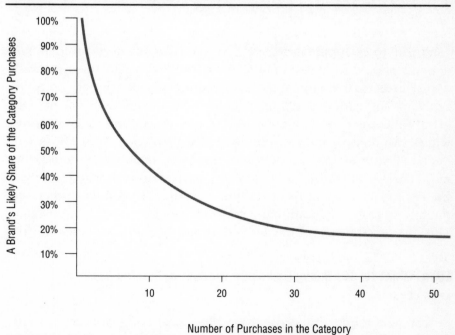

Source: Cartoonybin.com. Reproduced with permission.

"The pattern of apparent declining loyalty is largely a statistical artifact, dependent on the number of purchases used to calculate the measure."[23]

The fact is that larger purchase frequency in consumer goods typically means variety seeking, which offers the pleasure of novelty, even if the customer is highly loyal (e.g., a loyal Coca-Cola customer will occasionally drink a Sprite, and may even sometimes consume a Pepsi). That is simply a function of the number of purchase opportunities. And even in business-to-business relationships, high purchase frequency is likely to mean critical need for a product, which frequently makes single sourcing too risky or economically unsound. This, however, does not mean the customer is attitudinally less loyal.

LOYALTY MYTH 24: Heavy Users of a Product or Service Are Less Loyal

Researchers tend to report that it is light users of a product who are most loyal (i.e., they spend a higher percentage of their share-of-spending in the category on a single brand).[24] As discussed in the prior myth, however, it is obvious that a customer who purchases only once allocates 100 percent of his share-of-spending in the category to the brand. While behaviorally highly loyal, this customer would not easily qualify as a high-value customer.

Even though from a statistical perspective light buyers would seem likely to be classified as more loyal, this assumption does not survive a more rigorous analysis of purchase data. In fact, it turns out just the opposite is true. Stern and Hammond report that:

> . . . purchase weight (i.e., whether a buyer is a light, medium, or heavy purchaser of the category) affects share-based measures of loyalty. This seems to be a real effect rather than one determined by statistical artifact. The commonly reported finding that high loyalty tends to be driven by light buyers (who are perhaps 100 percent loyal because they make few purchases . . .) holds true only if the comparison is between light and heavy users in the same time period. If we compare brand loyalty across an equal number of purchases for light and heavy buyers (and therefore control for the small-number effect) we find that heavier buyers are more loyal.[25]

The reality is that heavy users appear more inclined to care about their relationship with a supplier than light users. Unfortunately, both managers and scientists are numbers-driven individuals, and on a circumspect review it could be said, "numbers don't lie." Maybe, but they certainly can be misinterpreted, as this myth clearly shows.

LOYALTY MYTH 25: The 50-Plus Age Segment Is More Loyal than Younger Segments

As any 50-plus aged television viewer can attest, the vast majority of television advertisements appear aimed at the under-50 consumer. For example, Procter & Gamble targets the 18- to 54-year old demographic for virtually every product category in which it has a product offering.[26]

Not surprisingly, people over 50 tend to be alienated by the age-biased advertising they see and hear. A survey of 30,000 over-50 consumers in the UK found that 70 percent believed their age group was not portrayed positively, and 74 percent reported they were completely unable to relate to television advertising.[27] To hammer home the same issue with U.S.-based advertisers, the American Association of Retired Persons (AARP) created an advertising campaign to overturn this bias. Aimed at marketing professionals, the advertisements ran in trade journals and cajoled marketers with provocative headlines like, "To Most Marketers, Consumers Die the Minute They Turn 50."

Part of the reason for advertising abandonment of 50-plus customers is that most of the creative people in advertising agencies are in their 20s and 30s, and therefore lack an empathy for older consumers. But the main reason 50-plus-year-olds aren't targeted is that they are falsely believed to be so entrenched in their buying habits that attempting to attract them is a wasted effort.

Source: Cartoonybin.com. Reproduced with permission.

Surprisingly, this commonly held belief has no basis in fact. A large-scale AARP study found that older consumers are just as likely to switch brands or experiment with alternative brands as are younger consumers. In other words, as Stephen Frost, research director for AARP Publications, proclaims, "Brand loyalty doesn't increase with age."[28]

LOYALTY MYTH 26: Loyal Customers Help Grow a Business Through Positive Word of Mouth

Word of mouth about products and services as a benefit of loyal customers is commonly held in high regard. The myth of its effectiveness has gained a big boost in management suites through two of the seminal loyalty publications:

1. The 1986 *Consumer Complaint Handling in America: An Update Study* published by the White House Office of Consumer Affairs stated that "On average, a dissatisfied customer will tell nine (9) people about their bad experience."[29]

2. Reichheld's and Sasser's 1990 *Harvard Business Review* article, "Zero Defections: Quality Comes to Services," proclaimed:

> Yet another economic boon from the long-time customer is the free advertising they provide. Loyal customers do a lot of talking over the years and drum up a lot of business. One of the leading home builders in the United States, for example, has found that more than 60 percent of its sales are the result of referrals."[30]

There is no question that for some business sectors, referrals are a major source of customer acquisition. But if it were more widespread, Reichheld and Sasser certainly would have offered a less obscure example in their article than that of "a leading home builder."

Customers tend to speak about products, services, and encounters with companies only in one of two extremes: extreme dissatisfaction, and extreme satisfaction (delight).[31] The problem is that customers are far more likely to speak about negative experiences than positive ones.[32]

As for loyal customers actively promoting a company through word of mouth, that depends upon how one defines loyalty. If we presume that loyalty is reflected in the tenure of customers with a firm, then the relationship between length of relationship and word of mouth is very weak. If we define loyalty as being attitudinally as well as behaviorally loyal, then customers' propensity to engage actively in word of mouth is markedly higher.[33]

But the impact of these word-of-mouth marketing efforts on customer acquisition is definitely overstated as it applies to most companies. Firms operating in areas where there is a perceived risk, status, or entertainment value associated with their products or services are much more likely to be impacted by word of mouth than firms offering less socially conspicuous products. Despite the dramatizations in "slice of life" advertising, people seldom ask one another, "Which toilet paper do you prefer?"

LOYALTY MYTH 27: Loyalty Can Be Measured by the Number of Net Promoters a Company Has

This is a relatively new myth, spawned by a 2003 *Harvard Business Review* article by Frederick Reichheld.[34] In essence, Reichheld argues that most of the effort that survey research companies expend to measure customer satisfaction and loyalty is wasted because they ask the wrong questions. Instead, he boldly asserts that the only question that needs to be asked is, "Would you recommend this company to a friend?"

Reichheld then argues that this response should be used to calculate the number of "net promoters" a firm has. Basically, he recommends asking the question on a 0 to 10 scale, where 10 means "extremely likely" and 0 means "not at all likely." He then calculates the proportion of brand users rating their likelihood of recommending it as a 9 or 10 (referred to as "promoters"), and subtracts from it the proportion rating their likelihood a 0 through 6 (referred to as "detractors"). And presto, one now has all the information needed from customers to grow a business—the proportion of "net promoters." Reichheld justifies his advocacy of this new measure by suggesting there are problems in correlating other measures with corporate profitability.

Reichheld's assertion that one only need collect a single measure to understand customer loyalty brings to mind a quote by the late Linus Pauling—the only person ever to have won two unshared Nobel Prizes: "The best way to have a good idea is to have a lot of ideas."[35] Reichheld is without question a thought leader in the customer loyalty community. Furthermore, the business community and the authors are in his debt for championing the importance of customer loyalty as a viable business strategy. However, in our opinion (and the opinion of the vast majority of marketing scientists), the concept of net promoters is a bad idea that would not likely have seen the light of day had it not come from such a respected individual. There are numerous problems with his proposed calculation.

First, the implication that all customer satisfaction and loyalty measurement systems fail to correlate with profits or growth is ridiculous. There are abundant scientific papers linking satisfaction and loyalty to financial outcomes for firms. For example, research has found that customer satisfaction has a measurable impact on purchase intentions,[36] on customer retention,[37] on financial performance,[38] and on word of mouth (a.k.a. likelihood of recommending).[39] Furthermore, researchers have found that companies that perform relatively better on the University of Michigan's American Customer Satisfaction Index (ACSI) produce significantly more "market value added" (a cumulative measure of corporate performance reflecting the difference between what investors have put in and what they can take out).[40] This documented relationship between stock market performance and firm growth directly contradicts Reichheld's assertions.

Second, even if the "net promoter" concept correctly measured a firm's customer loyalty level (which it does not), it doesn't give managers a clue as to what they should do. Instead of being a guide to action, it is simply a temperature reading. Imagine a doctor taking your child's temperature, announcing that he has a high fever, and saying, "He's definitely ill, good luck." Only by understanding what actually drives customer loyalty can managers effectively prioritize their improvement efforts—and this requires a great deal more diagnostic information from customers than simply their likelihood to recommend a firm to a friend.

Third, Reichheld seems to have quite unusual data. He contends that the "net promoter" score is independent of other measures (satisfaction and loyalty). It is hard to imagine a scenario in which customers' overall satisfaction levels, their likelihood to repurchase, and their likelihood to recommend the firm were not all highly correlated (assuming that they were asked these things in the same questionnaire, using a similar response scale). In numerous studies the authors have conducted, the measures of customer satisfaction, repurchase intention, and the likelihood of recommending have always been found to be highly correlated, at a level of 0.8 or better.

That one of these questions might perform better than the others when relating them to firm growth is possible, even probable, given that the correlation among the measures is not perfect. But to assert that the "likelihood to recommend" measure works well while customer satisfaction does not is beyond credibility given their generally high inter-correlation. Perhaps Reichheld's data (not shown in his *HBR* article) actually support such a conclusion. But given that

Source: Cartoonybin.com. Reproduced with permission.

some of the best marketing scientists in the world have extensively examined this area and compiled a vast amount of research, one would expect Reichheld's assertions to have been corroborated by at least one of them through their own research; to date there is no corroboration.

Fourth, and probably most damning, is that, as we find in the answer to the prior myth, loyal customers don't always act as advocates for brands, services, and companies. So if the presence of word of mouth is actually more constrained than conventionally thought, how exactly does the "net promoter" concept work?

LOYALTY MYTH 28: Loyal Customers Will Work to Establish a Relationship

Personal relationships are two-way streets that demand give-and-take from each participant in order for them to thrive. Firm-customer relationships, however, are not on par with the usual bonds between people. Regardless of the intensity of the affiliation, a customer is still a customer. He is paying to get a want or need fulfilled by a product, service, or firm. In other words, the customer is paying for a solution to his problem.

As a result, customers typically are not willing to expend further effort beyond the level required to complete a business transaction. Therefore, putting too much onus on the customer to enhance the relationship is likely an exercise in futility. The customer is still king. And when the rules of loyalty programs are changed (as frequently happens), the most likely result will be disillusioned, once-loyal customers. The net result? An erosion of the loyalty the program was instituted to enhance.

Nordstrom discovered this the hard way. As the *Wall Street Journal* reported, "With hip-hop music and flashing lights, Nordstrom has been trying to get shoppers to trade tweed blazers for leather miniskirts. Ads have been urging customers, 'Reinvent Yourself.' "[41] The problem was that customers liked things the way they were. Sales slipped badly. As a result, chairman and CEO John Whitacre, the first person outside the Nordstrom family ever to hold those titles, is now the *former* chairman and CEO.

The only relationship work a loyal customer might be willing to undertake is overlooking a service failure. Some emotionally loyal customers will even exert the effort to alert a company to a service or process failure, out of their commitment to the company. It's a pity that far too few companies have processes in place to actually attend to complaints and act on them. Truly, a complaint can be a gift, but only if one has the resources to attend to the complaints and fix them.

SETTING THE RECORD STRAIGHT ABOUT CUSTOMERS: THEIR NEEDS, BEHAVIORS, AND REFERRALS

Most of what we have been told about how customer loyalty impacts customer behavior is either only occasionally right or never right. Yet, as customers ourselves, we recognize that we tend to spend more on products and services to which we feel a degree of loyalty. The problem is that in many categories, as consumers we fail to see a benefit in having a relationship and we're unwilling to invest our efforts to form one. Even where we might desire a relationship, we seldom see a benefit for us in committing to a monogamous relationship with a firm.

These two facts have a cascading impact on virtually all other behaviors associated with customer loyalty. For example, if we are loyal to multiple firms, how does that influence our word of mouth? And if we don't seek a relationship with a firm, then how likely are we even to seek a recommendation?

Understanding the real impact of enhancing customer loyalty on customer behavior is essential to determining the appropriateness of any loyalty effort. Otherwise, customers may feel more loyal to your brand but still not change their spending.

Loyalty Truth 3: Focus on customers' share-of-wallet. Don't disregard those customers with current low shares; consumer polygamy is the rule these days. But don't accept your current share. Learn how to improve your share of your customers' loyalty.

It's important to differentiate repeat purchasing from true loyalty. Loyalty is mitigated by the involvement customers feel with products and services. Rarely will customers invest much effort in building a relationship. Customers will only engage in monogamous relationships for categories of extreme importance; in other situations they'll act defensively by being polygamous. But there is still value in the share of loyalty they accord your company or brand.

CHAPTER 4

Loyalty Myths Concerning Loyalty Programs

Source: Cartoonybin.com. Reproduced with permission.

Most customer loyalty programs are unthinking imitations of other programs. They aren't aligned with the particular needs and interests of customers at all. As a result, there is no differentiation among competitive programs, nor reasons for customers to care. In typical "me-too" behavior, companies follow one another like lemmings off a cliff, taking comfort in the fact that everyone else went with them.[1]

—Servet Topaloğlu, CEO, Tansaş

THE PARABLE OF PLASTIC LOYALTY

In March 2002, Servet Topaloğlu (Toh-pal-O-loo), CEO and vice chairman of the board of Turkish grocery retailer Tansaş, was faced with a grim picture: losses of more than $100 million and a market share that did not reflect the potential of the company. Losses were common for the chain. Just three months earlier Tansaş had hired Topaloğlu away from the Real chain (Metro Group's German hypermarket chain), where he had served as CEO for five years. His assignment was to turn Tansaş around.

Making Tansaş a success, however, would prove to be a daunting task. Tansaş was not the preferred supermarket chain of many Turkish consumers.

Tansaş had tried all the right things, including a loyalty card program. The program, driven by purchase data from its one million members, aimed to provide promotions and personalized offerings. But it simply was not working. One of the problems was that most Turkish consumers had a variety of supermarket loyalty cards; their wallets were stuffed. Investigating the situation further, under Topaloğlu's direction, Tansaş executives learned that there was no difference in profitability, frequency of visit, or loyalty between those of its customers who belonged to its program and those who did not. Obviously, the conventional loyalty card and the store's positioning of it were not providing solutions to increase the chain's low market share.

Topaloğlu, an engineer by training, realized that reengineering Tansaş was going to require more than an operations overhaul; it was going to demand a unique proposition that allowed customers to believe that the Tansaş chain deserved their loyalty. He arrived at a radical solution: a shopping experience designed to appeal to all of a customer's senses, anchored by a written "Incredible Consumer Rights" statement from Tansaş—literally a customer's "Bill of Rights"—establishing Tansaş customers' expectations, while offering competitive prices compared to other chains.

Having the vision, Topaloğlu had to convince Tansaş board members to buy in. "I knew immediately that this was not the strategy that the board had envisioned I would propose when I was hired," recalls Topaloğlu. "But I knew that we had to give consumers a clear and differentiating reason to choose Tansaş." Not surprisingly, opposing board members were neither hesitant in voicing their objections nor restrained with their criticisms, but after a long and often tense debate, Topaloğlu managed to dispel the board members' concerns. He emphasized the importance of building the necessary supply chain, conducting employee training, renegotiating vendor contracts, and deploying a creative advertising campaign for the successful implementation of the strategy. "Although many were legitimately skeptical when we began our meeting," notes Topaloğlu, "by the end of the meeting, all were convinced and committed!"

The first step was the formulation of a plan to implement the in-store experience. Topaloğlu believed that this experience needed to appeal to the five senses. The new concept organized the store such that arriving customers would be greeted with appetizing, freshly baked bread aromas from the bakery section. Walking past the bakery, customers would be attracted to the vegetable and fruit section by a mélange of colors and shapes. New age music composed specially for Tansaş would sooth consumers for the duration of their shopping trip, ensuring their shopping would be as peaceful and relaxing as possible. Store public address systems were turned off, so as not to interrupt shoppers with shrill announcements. The overall aim was to make sure customers thoroughly enjoyed their Tansaş shopping experience.

The next step was to formulate the "Incredible Consumers Rights" policy. The genesis of the policy was an extensive research study that asked consumers from a diverse set of demographic profiles what they hated most about supermarket shopping. Research findings provided the building blocks for the promises that constitute the "Incredible Consumer Rights" philosophy at Tansaş today:

1. *Return guarantee on all food items.* All returned unsatisfactory food items, regardless of whether they are partially consumed, shall be accepted, no questions asked.

2. *Out-of-stock guarantee for promotional items.* Any item on promotion, if out of stock, shall be replaced by an equal- or higher-value product in the same category for the price of the promotion item.

3. *Freshness guarantee.* Should any item with an expired consumption date be found on store shelves, a fresh replacement of this item will be given to the consumer free of charge.

4. *Insurance guarantee.* Tansaş customers shall be insured against accidents that may occur inside the store and potential health problems caused by food items acquired from Tansaş stores.

5. *Price guarantee.* Should the labeled price be different than the one that appears at the cash register, the lower price shall be effective.

6. *Printing error guarantee.* Should the price of a product announced be lower than its actual price due to a printing error, the lower price shall be effective at cash registers.

7. *Food safety guarantee.* Food items that do not have manufacturing permits cannot be sold at Tansaş. All products shall be regularly audited by TÜBİTAK (The Scientific and Technical Research Council of Turkey) for food safety. (This may not appear to be a significant issue to some, but there are some food processors and other supermarket chains in Turkey that do not adhere to the TÜBİTAK standard. Tansaş

is making a statement that the health of its customers is paramount.)

8. *Cash register availability guarantee.* Customers shall have the right to request a cash register be opened should there be a queue at other registers. Should an idle cash register not be made available within three minutes of the request, the first 20 million Turkish liras (approximately $15) of the purchase will be free![2]

Finally, an extensive advertising campaign was undertaken to create awareness of the new Tansaş positioning and store concept. An advertising agency was retained to create a campaign to communicate the new image and offer. In addition, a public relations firm was hired to conduct an effective PR program.

Tansaş used its unique return policy to effectively differentiate itself in the minds of Turkish consumers. In the UK, the Tesco chain had depicted a similar exchange policy through now-famous television commercials. In one of these Tesco ads, a little girl returns a fish her mother bought to the Tesco salesperson because the fish is not smiling. The seafood clerk takes the fish back—no questions asked—and points the little girl to an array of other fish so that she may choose one that is smiling.

Tansaş's real-life experience with its exchange policy generated a collection of no less memorable anecdotes. One story involves a middle-aged man who asked to return a half-finished bottle of Raki (a local alcoholic drink) because it made him drunk. Another involved a woman who received reimbursement for the detergent she purchased to clean her carpet, stained by the difficult-to-handle, "defectively-shaped watermelon" purchased from Tansaş.

Consumer perceptions were monitored vigilantly by the Retailing Institute of Turkey. The November 2004 results showed that after the makeover and launch of the communications campaign, perceptions corresponded to those envisioned for the company, significantly enhancing the company's image vis-à-vis its competitors. Figure 4.1 shows how customers rated Tansaş on each of 20 perceptions, relative to its best scoring competitor.

FIGURE 4.1 Tansaş Performance Chart

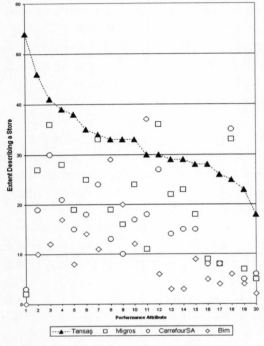

Performance Attributes

1 Closed cash register is opened within 3 minutes.
2 Food quality assurance.
3 Cleanliness of store environment.
4 What I pay at the register is the same as that on the price label.
5 As a consumer, I believe my rights are protected.
6 Friendly store personnel.
7 I can find what I am looking for easily.
8 Easily accessible.
9 Payment without much waiting in cash register queues.
10 I do not come across products with expired "best before" dates.
11 Reasonable prices.
12 Contemporary, modern and young families shop here.
13 Product quality of meat and dairy products.
14 Product quality of vegetables and fruits.
15 I do not experience problems with product returns.
16 Should a printing error occur, the lower price is effective.
17 Any item on promotion, if out-of-stock, is replaced by an equal or higher value product in the same category for the price of the promotion item.
18 Product variety/assortment.
19 A fresh replacement of any expired item is given free of charge.
20 I am insured during my shopping.

Source: Tansaş internal documents. *Source of data:* Tansaş Advertising Campaign Post Test Study conducted by Retailing Institute, Istanbul, Turkey, November 2004.

The Moral of Plastic Loyalty

Tansaş has been widely praised for its strategy and has received an impressive list of awards. Turkey's Ministry of Industry, Trade, and Commerce awarded Tansaş the Traditional Consumer Award three times, which recognizes a "company that adopts customer satisfaction as a business philosophy." The company won the national Consumer Quality Award, and *Consumer Reports* in Turkey recognized Tansaş with its Golden Quality Award for Consumer Friendliness.

All these awards would be hollow if they were not accompanied by positive financial results. From the inception of the program in 2002 until end of fiscal year 2004, Tansaş transformed its more than

$100 million loss into record and unrivaled growth in revenues: from $371 million in 2002 to $700 million by the end of 2004. Tansaş's growth is not the result of more stores being opened; the increased revenue came from more customers adopting Tansaş as their preferred store and spending more with Tansaş.[3] The average number of customers per day shopping at Tansaş stores increased from 179,000 to 209,000 within just over a year after the strategy was implemented, and the amount spent per customer increased by 11 percent over the same time period. And it was all done with the same number of employees, indirectly making a strategy designed to improve customers' shopping experiences a productivity improvement policy as well. As a result, Tansaş has become one of the most profitable local retail supermarket chains in Turkey, with 201 stores and close to 5,000 employees.

Tansaş's experience demonstrates that a loyalty card program lacking definitive benefits does not by itself ensure customer loyalty. As Topaloğlu avows, "The success of Tansaş is a testimony to the

Source: Cartoonybin.com. Reproduced with permission.

loyalty of our customers. But to earn that loyalty, we had to recognize that receiving customer loyalty is about giving customers a reason to believe that Tansaş *deserves* their loyalty."

For too many retailers, customer loyalty strategies are little more than adopting a frequent shopper program, which is still perceived as a panacea. We have already established that to receive loyalty from customers, a business has to understand which customers it wants to retain and what it can uniquely offer these customers to build their loyalty. The loyalty program should also be in sync with the company's strategy and, unlike Tansaş's original loyalty card program, deliver bottom-line results. But loyalty programs are replete with money-draining false promises, often improperly executed and shortsighted. What follows are the most frequently asserted myths surrounding loyalty programs, and their lesser known realities.

LOYALTY MYTH 29: Loyalty Programs Are a Sound Investment

If the only source of information you had on loyalty programs were the sales materials from vendors who coordinate such programs, you would be tempted to consider them a fail-safe road to riches. Despite their popularity among chain stores, and quite contrary to popular belief, most loyalty programs actually lose money for their sponsors!

The economics of these frequently touted remedies just don't make sense. Loyalty programs are expensive to create and maintain, and they often produce disastrous returns. A study by McKinsey & Company found that investments in these programs, including IT, training, and so on, can cost large retailers up to $30 million in the first year, and annual maintenance costs can total $5 to $10 million a year thereafter. This requires a store-by-store increase in sales of about 6 percent, on average, just to break even on the costs of the program. For most retailers, this is an unattainable same-store-sales growth rate. The probability of recovering these costs seems bleak, particularly given the fickleness of many consumers regarding their choice of retailer.[4] The results for casual apparel retailers seem particularly discouraging: up to 79 percent of customers say they frequently consider changing retailers.

Obtaining a positive ROI becomes less viable given that the vast majority of loyalty programs do not contribute to increased sales. Although this phenomenon is more pervasive in some retail categories than others, consumers who have a loyalty card do not seem to end up spending much more than those who do not. In the grocery industry, customers who are members of a loyalty program spend 48 percent more than customers who are not members, but this figure drops to 18 percent in the casual apparel retail category. Although loyalty cardholders tend to spend more than noncardholders, even in the grocery category there is the issue of causality: Do frequent shoppers decide to sign up for the program because they are rewarded for doing something they would do anyway? Likely a large percentage of loyalty card customers—possibly the vast majority—are accumulating points or discounts without having changed their purchasing behavior from before they were members.

The Fly Buy loyalty program is an excellent case of loyalty programs not altering spending. Fly Buy had the largest per capita market coverage loyalty program in Australia and was at one point responsible for 20 percent of all retail spending in Australia. It had more than two million members two years after its launch and an operating budget in excess of $20 million.[5] The loyalty program was based on earning points for shopping at certain department stores and supermarkets, using credit cards, and purchasing gasoline. The points could later be redeemed for free air travel and accommodations. There was, however, no evidence to demonstrate the effectiveness of this program.

Researchers Byron and Anne Sharp set out to explore the program's effectiveness using consumer panel data to model deviations from regular purchase patterns attributable to the Fly Buy loyalty program.[6] Their review yielded two main conclusions: (1) There was no evidence that Fly Buy brands experienced increased purchase frequencies when purchase patterns were analyzed; and (2) "out of the six Fly Buy brands, only two showed substantial repeat purchase loyalty," which applied to both Fly Buy members and nonmembers. Given the amount of consumer involvement in this loyalty program, its failure to achieve substantial increases in loyalty is discouraging, and clearly points to the lack of understanding regarding what loyalty really is, how it is created, and how it is maintained.

Demand for such programs is also often not precisely estimated, resulting in some terrifying so-called successes, as the sponsors of LatinPass discovered. LatinPass (now GlobalPass) is a frequent-flier program consortium of several Latin American airlines. In January 2000 it offered a one-million-mile bonus to customers who, by July 1, 2000, flew at least one international segment on each of its member airlines, plus took three flights on partner carriers, stayed three nights in partner hotels, and rented a car for five days from a partner rental agency. Unfortunately, LatinPass failed to estimate the attractiveness of earning a million miles. The promotion sparked unprecedented interest. It was widely discussed on Internet message boards visited by mileage chasers. The premium was apparently so unique that word traveled even into the United States, where the network news program *The Today Show* mentioned the one-million-mile promotion. Committed mileage chasers designed itineraries that would let them fulfill the requirements in only three and a half days. As a result, by March 20, 2000, LatinPass officials had to close the program to new members and restrict it to only current card-carrying program members.

Although LatinPass successfully restricted redemption to existing members, frequently amending a loyalty program can not only disturb customer trust but can also be expensive. For example, in February 2000, a rule was inserted in the LatinPass promotion program in fine print that forbade the transfer of miles via the Hilton HHonors' Reward Exchange. This action created a great deal of anger among members. After several complaints, LatinPass rescinded the rule. But LatinPass underestimated the attractiveness of miles and could not live up to its promise.[7] Depending on how the LatinPass points were redeemed, it could cost the operators of the program between $5,000 and $10,000 per million-mile recipient—meaning that LatinPass lost a lot of money on the promotion.[8]

Other well-known frequent-flier programs also provide striking examples. American Airlines' AAdvantage program was the first airline frequent-flier program. Since its introduction in 1981 participation has grown from 750,000 members to about 40 million. (Interestingly, the program was originally conceived not as a loyalty program but rather as a mechanism by which the airline could identify who was sitting in its seats—at the time the preponderance of airline tickets were sold by travel agents who didn't report to the airlines on the identities of purchasers. With such a large customer base and responsibility, even the slightest changes to the rules have been known to bring massive class action suits. When American Airlines attempted to alter the terms of its program, it ended up having to settle legal claims by offering millions of dollars in mileage credit and fare discounts. Delta Air Lines settled a similar lawsuit in 1998.[9]

Therefore, while it is possible that a loyalty program can be a good financial investment, the probability that any one program will be successful is slim given the numerous pitfalls.

LOYALTY MYTH 30: The Tools for Building Loyalty Are Well Understood and Practiced

Customer loyalty is a combination of customers' attitudes and their behaviors. Professor Richard Oliver sums up loyalty this way: "[Loyalty is] a deeply held commitment to re-buy or re-patronize a preferred product/service consistently in the future, thereby causing repetitive same brand or same brand-set purchasing, despite situational influences and marketing efforts having the potential to cause switching behavior"[10] Oliver goes on to propose four different levels of loyalty:

1. Conative loyalty: loyalty to information such as prices, features, and so on.
2. Affective loyalty: loyalty to a liking (i.e., I buy it because I like it).
3. Cognitive loyalty: loyalty to an intention (i.e., I'm committed to buying it).
4. Action loyalty: loyalty to action (i.e., inertia, coupled with the overcoming of obstacles).

Given this multilevel definition of loyalty, how many products can we list for which this level of commitment is evidenced? Probably very few, because many product categories are plagued by variety-seeking behavior and are therefore susceptible to frequent switching.

Designing an effective loyalty program requires that companies deciding to use one must have a model of loyalty in mind and should have identified the drivers of loyalty among their customers. Most programs directed at engendering high levels of loyalty demonstrate obvious limitations in their understanding of the true meaning of loyalty. Loyalty programs often do not generate increased purchases because most people generally buy only what they need.

Researchers Bolton, Kannan, and Bramlet found that 43 percent of customers did not use their loyalty-building credit card during the one-year study period; a further 36 percent used their card on fewer than six occasions. No program that results in 79 percent of its members using the card infrequently or not at all can be described as particularly motivating.[11] There are similar findings in the retail sector. Researchers Wright and Sparks[12] found that as many as a fifth of retail loyalty cardholders did not make any use of their card over a three-month period. In general, enhancing the bond between customers and their brands and expecting that this will automatically stimulate more demand for the product category is neither reasonable nor sustainable.[13] Ultimately, customers will settle to a state of purchasing only what they need, when they truly need it.

Understanding how consumers prefer their loyalty rewarded is also a key component of designing effective programs. Typically, customers become frustrated with the time it takes to build the necessary stature to be eligible for rewards. When consumers leave a loyalty or rewards program, most (70 percent) cite the length of time it takes to build up points as the most important reason. This number jumps to 79 percent in the critical 18 to 24 age group. Other causes of customer defection included the following:

▮ Not being rewarded properly (23 percent).

▮ Disliked the fee (22 percent).

▮ Disliked the reward options (20 percent).

▮ Program rules kept changing (17 percent).

■ Poor customer service (16 percent).

■ Other programs seemed better (18 percent).[14]

No doubt the rate at which points are collected depends directly on how much is spent. It was found that high-income individuals ($125,000 or more) spend more money and collect points at a faster rate, but, compared with other customers, they are fussy and more likely to comparison shop. More than one quarter (27 percent) of this demographic group left a rewards program because another company's program seemed better or they did not like the reward options.[15]

The most frequently used tool for addressing customer loyalty is a frequent shopper program. From the Dunkin' Donuts "Buy 12 dozen, get the 13th free" to Harrah's Casinos' "Total Rewards Program," the emphasis of such programs is a reward for frequency of purchase. Although these programs may have their place, their use in building

Source: Cartoonybin.com. Reproduced with permission.

genuine customer loyalty is limited. As the success of Tansaş demonstrates, you have to give customers a reason to believe that you *deserve* their loyalty, and this is rarely accomplished by a points program; worse still for managers, it is rarely a solution, either.

LOYALTY MYTH 31: Loyalty Can't Be Bought, It Has to Be Earned

The idea that loyalty cannot be bought is really a function of how one defines loyalty. If, as with most consumer packaged goods, loyalty is defined as the share-of-spending in the category, then loyalty not only can be bought, but frequently is. The head of direct response marketing for a large retail firm lamented, "We have trained our loyal customers to [delay shopping, to] wait for our coupon in the mail." He was frustrated to find that when the firm tested the program by not sending the coupon one month, sales plummeted. "We have to learn to wean them off of the 'drug.'" This is a prevalent situation for many firms. We train customers to wait for deals, resulting in huge spikes in sales with every promotional effort and weak sales in off-promotion periods.

Managers are so conditioned to giving products and services away to get sales that we frequently find tragicomedies of loyalty programs similar to the LatinPass fiasco. For example, much of the world has already heard of the "pudding guy," David Phillips, the 35-year-old Davis, California, engineer who earned 1.25 million frequent-flier miles by cleverly exploiting a Healthy Choice promotion that offered air miles for product purchases. Phillips ended up with $25,000 to $75,000 in free travel by spending only $3,140 on pudding cups, the least expensive product in Healthy Choice's brand family. Phillips achieved this remarkable reward by figuring out a way to earn 100 American Airlines frequent-flier miles for each 25-cent cup of pudding he purchased. He ended up with 1.2 million air miles—worth 48 free domestic airline tickets—and 12,000 desserts. Why did he do it? " 'I always look for something for nothing, or as cheap as possible,' says Phillips. 'I started by wanting some free tickets to Europe for my family, but as I got deeper into the frequent-flier deals and saw the opportunities, I decided to pull out all the stops. For example, many people were into the Healthy Choice promotion, but they only bought the amount of food that they could eat in a several-year period. The idea of donating the food I bought was what separated me from the others.' "[16]

Although the pudding guy could be cited as an extreme example of a loyalty program hacker, there are many instances when customers buy the products solely to build financial rewards or exploit the system. Both the Healthy Choice and the LatinPass programs were easily exploitable. The result? In such cases firms are merely buying the repeat purchases of customers rather than developing true loyalty. Said another way, most loyalty programs try to hold the customer hostage instead of nurturing loyalty. In such situations, customers are likely to invest their time and effort in becoming a member. They later may be driven by the sunk-cost fallacy, where they are motivated to continue by thinking of how much they have

Source: Cartoonybin.com. Reproduced with permission.

already accumulated rather than more realistically focusing on how much more they have to accumulate to reach an award plateau. Hence, they become locked into the program and continued interaction, despite the fact that they may not feel truly (attitudinally) loyal.

LOYALTY MYTH 32: Frequency of Contact Increases Loyalty

This myth stems from an observed phenomenon, namely, for most business categories, the most loyal customers tend to be the most active customers; loyalty is often correlated with more frequent interactions with the firm. As a result, firms have actively sought to reward customers for their purchase frequency in the hopes of generating greater customer loyalty. The problem is a chicken-and-egg conundrum. Do frequent purchases create loyalty, or does loyalty generate more frequent purchases? The disappointing truth is that attitudinal loyalty most often leads to frequent purchasing, not the other way around.

Although there are exceptions, most loyalty programs are really bribes to increase customers' frequency of interaction. For example, retailers commonly put different items on sale exclusively for loyalty cardholders on a weekly basis. This means customers are being rewarded for more frequent or higher purchases, but it does not necessarily mean that they are loyal. The company may in fact be rewarding the wrong type of behavior—one that can actually hurt its bottom line. If customers spend about the same total amount but increase their frequency of contact, transaction costs are increased while revenues remain constant. The result is lower gross profits even before the costs of the program are factored in. And, as we noted in myth 30, ultimately, customers will settle back into a state of purchasing what they actually need.

LOYALTY MYTH 33: Loyalty Can Be Created through Economic or Structural Bonds

Without question, behavioral loyalty can be enhanced (or even required) through economic or structural bonds. We have all heard something equivalent to "I fly ABC Airlines because it is the only carrier with direct routes from X to Y." That does not mean the customer would not switch if given the opportunity; in fact, he may pray for such an opportunity to arise. As many firms in recently deregulated industries throughout the United States and Europe have discovered (for example, telecommunications and airlines), holding customers hostage does not equal customer loyalty. The goal of most loyalty programs is to create a structural bond with the firm. In some cases this can work, but, as noted in myth 30, most programs do not provide an offer compelling enough for the vast majority of customers to alter their behavior significantly.

Furthermore, most loyalty programs are indiscriminate in their targeting of customers. Remember that the vast majority of customers do not provide an acceptable rate of return for most firms, and creating structural bonds with the wrong customers is a poor business strategy. Enrique Felgueres, CEO of travel web site Viajo.com, lamented, "The LatinPass program did not produce Latin American business executives who are obsessive collectors of travel miles. I don't have a single client who uses LatinPass. Some use the Aeromexico pass, but the mileage frenzy is principally a U.S. phenomenon. Airline loyalty programs can be useful for some Latin American travelers but, overall, passengers don't benefit because once you earn your awards, there's always the issue that you can't use them."[17]

The strongest bonds are a combination of structure and emotion, whether in business or in our personal lives (that is, we tend to be closest to those who share similar interests and pursuits). But structural bonds without emotional ties tend to be easily broken when the opportunity arises. Firms forget this at their long-term peril. The combination of capitalism, competition, and democracy ensures that competitive environments will always move toward more choices for customers. Relationships of convenience forced by structural ties will tend to erode, but emotional ties are not easily displaced.

LOYALTY MYTH 34: Loyalty Rewards Programs Will Solve Customer Attrition Problems

As noted in the Introduction, one of the primary appeals of customer loyalty as a business strategy is to counter the epidemic of customer churn

Source: Cartoonybin.com. Reproduced with permission.

in many industries. Loyalty programs are specifically aimed at solving these problems—it is in the sales materials of program vendors:

- ▋ "Maximize your customer retention at a minimum cost."[18]
- ▋ "Yes, I want to increase revenue and boost repeat purchase at no cost to me!"[19]
- ▋ "Promote customer retention . . . Avoid customer defection."[20]

Regardless of whether the statements of these various loyalty program providers are true, they most definitely assume one thing: The firm's product or service does not stink. Even if we assume that a well-designed and differentiated loyalty program can enhance loyalty, a loyalty program cannot save a bad product. Think about it in the extreme: If an airline consistently canceled your flights, would frequent-flier miles really matter?

Worse still, problems with loyalty programs can exacerbate customer attrition problems. According to a recent study by *Frequent Flyer* magazine of air travelers' satisfaction with different aspects of air travel, consumers ranked frequent-flier programs at the bottom, just ahead of airline food.[21] Unfortunately, there are too many award miles chasing a fixed and far smaller number of award seats on most airlines' flights. Travelers are often refused a free ticket or upgrade for their preferred flight at the time of year and on the day they want. Program members are forced into compromises such as scheduling their award trips at inconvenient times of day, or taking several connecting flights rather than the quicker nonstops. Or they cannot schedule their travel at all.[22] All the less reason to stay loyal!

LOYALTY MYTH 35: Loyalty Programs Will Attract Customers from Competitors

If a firm was already competitively positioned in its market and somehow was the only one in its category to offer a loyalty program, it probably could attract customers. That, however, is not the case in virtually any market on the planet. The proliferation of loyalty programs makes differentiation and, hence, the ability to attract customers from competitors difficult, if not impossible. For example, an estimated 92 million travelers (73 percent of them American) are members of at least one of the 90 worldwide frequent-flier programs. Many Americans belong to five or more. According to OAG's 1997 "Business Lifestyle Survey" of 5,000 frequent travelers in the United States, Britain, France, Germany, Italy, Singapore, Hong Kong, Japan, and Australia, 9 out of 10 business travelers were found to be frequent-flier program members. The more they travel, the more programs they belong to.[23] And customers see little difference between various loyalty programs. As noted in the Introduction, research into hotel frequent guest programs found that once the branding and logos were removed from the rewards catalogues, members failed to recognize differences between competing programs. Similarly, most airline travelers believe there are scarce differences, if any, between various airlines' frequent-flier programs.[24] The ubiquity and lack of perceived differentiation of these programs makes attracting customers from competitors based solely on the virtues of the loyalty program unachievable.

LOYALTY MYTH 36: The Internet Makes Building Loyalty Much Easier

The Internet can make communication of information between company and customer immediate and, possibly, personal; however, overall it is more likely to weaken customer loyalty. The Internet makes information widely available and, therefore, a comparison of competing goods much easier. The existence of comparison sites such as mysimon.com and bizrate.com greatly enhances customers' ability to acquire perfect product and price information at minimal effort and cost. This ultimately leads to increased consumer price sensitivity. Results of a study that asked a group of people to search for wine using online comparison agents like those mentioned previously confirmed this point. Providing comparison agents lowered search costs for quality information and led to consumers' increased price sensitivity regarding wine.[25]

This phenomenon has been exacerbated with the introduction of smart recommendation agents—essentially electronic algorithms that act like online salespeople. The interactive nature of the online environment enables consumers to specify a set of preferences that are then used to compile a list of recommended products. Smart agents screen a universe of alternatives, recommending only a limited number that are well matched to the customer's preferences. Such agents have been found to contribute to increased price sensitivity by making it easier to conduct more focused product comparisons.[26] The reduced cost of acquiring information has also increased consumers' product choices. With access to a greater portfolio of choices, and lower costs to switch brands compared to a traditional brick-and-mortar retailer, customers lack sufficient incentives to maintain a monogamous relationship with any single retailer.

These factors negatively correlate with the ease with which e-loyalty is presumed to be built and maintained. Contrary to common belief, customer acquisition and retention are more difficult in the Internet environment. Compared to traditional retailers, customer acquisition costs are 20 to 40 percent higher for pure-play Web companies (retailers existing solely on the Internet).[27] Electronic retailers also find that it takes much longer to observe returns on these acquisition expenditures. Web relationships typically take two to three years to break even, in part because customer attrition rates are significantly higher: Up to 50 percent of customers defect within the first three years. Electronic loyalty appears to be fundamentally different from the off-line environment. The promise of the Internet is one-to-one, near immediate, personalized communication (which may eventually come to pass), but the immediate benefit for customers is the ability to quickly and accurately compare a large number of competing products, which almost certainly fosters brand switching.

SETTING THE RECORD STRAIGHT: LOYALTY PROGRAM MYTHS

Most of us, like the Turkish consumers Tansaş was appealing to, are members of multiple loyalty programs. Yet almost everybody would admit that loyalty programs are not a big driver of chosen relationships. If the sponsoring product or service failed to deliver, we would shop somewhere else. The failure of these programs is in their lack of differentiation and their lack of true value. Not only do we perceive little value in their benefits or rewards, but we also recognize we could receive identical or similar rewards from numerous other programs. They lack the kind of added value that we could expect to receive through only one specific program. With these failures identified, it is easy to see why many loyalty programs are just not working.

Some do work, of course. A few loyalty programs may even offer a rarified virtual country club. Leading Hotels of the World's "Leaders Club" program targets affluent individuals who stay more than 60 nights a year in a luxury hotel. Basic membership is free to frequent guests of the association's worldwide properties; higher tiers offering more benefits are offered at between $300 and $1,000 per year. Leading Hotels of the World reports that the 90,000 members of its Leaders Club find the exclusivity of the program the most appealing aspect.[28]

So what is the key for programs to successfully create loyalty? Here are nine dimensions identified by researchers O'Brien and Jones.

1. An underlying product or service that provides value is a prerequisite to creating loyalty to the brand; loyalty programs won't salvage an inferior product.

2. For some products, because of the nature of the category, monogamous loyalty is just not attainable by loyalty programs.

3. The loyalty program must be carefully designed and ROI forecasted accurately. Changes made to the program *after* the launch can and will cause trouble.

4. The customer must perceive value in the loyalty program or it will not work.

5. Giving choice to customers about how they want to use their rewards is critical.

6. Providing value other than monetary value (aspirational value) can be a valuable tool in building true loyalty.

7. Rewards need to be relevant to the customer.

8. Convenience should be provided in redeeming rewards.

9. Communication of the program to customers needs to be properly done.[29]

Most programs fail to deliver on most or all of the above. Even those programs that aspire to these standards would be hard-pressed to keep from being rapidly copied. For now, most loyalty programs are no more than a means of achieving parity with competition— which is another way of saying they're adding costs to the business without adding revenue.

Loyalty Truth 4: Loyalty requires mutually beneficial interaction; most loyalty programs are tilted in the company's favor.

A compelling loyalty offer must be based on mutual benefit: a real benefit for the customer as well as the benefit of customer retention for the sponsoring organization. Customers must be given as much satisfaction through their relationships as the marketer receives from their loyal patronage. There was a five-year period when (according to the authors' observations) coupons for discount automotive oil change service had become the currency of loyalty in the United States; that is, nearly every loyalty program offered discount oil change coupons as a reward. Why any organization thought that offering its customers a discount on another company's service could be interpreted as a tangible benefit is hard to understand. Obviously, the oil change service was actively promoting its coupons to major marketing organizations, and many accepted the offer.

If you look to a loyalty program as a point of competitive difference, make sure you offer rewards or benefits that, for your desirable customers, are:

▌ Meaningful.

▌ Perceived as real value added.

▌ Relevant to or consistent with your products and services.

Rewards should never disparage or denigrate the value of the core offering. Ideal rewards are those that tie into the sponsor's product or service or enhance its use—for example, providing a DVD cleaning pad or storage shelf when a critical number of DVDs are purchased. Far too many organizations use economic bonds like "after four purchases you receive a 10 percent discount" or "buy 12 dozen and your next dozen is free." These incentives can backfire, causing customers to question the value of the product at its everyday price.

CHAPTER 5

Loyalty Myths about Loyalty, Share of Business, and Profitability

We've found that there's a direct correlation between customer loy-
alty, employee engagement, and bottom-line profitability in terms
of our stores.[1]

—Al Lenzmeier, vice chairman, Best Buy

The mid-1990s was a period of extreme turmoil for the European telecommunications industry, but perhaps none of the affected telecommunications companies faced greater obstacles than France Télécom. The enterprise was a government monopoly facing the opportunity for privatization but confronted by the likely entry of competitors for the first time in its history.

THE PARABLE OF PAYING TOO MUCH FOR CUSTOMER LOYALTY

January 1, 1998 was the deadline imposed for opening the telecommunications industries in Europe. Unfortunately, every time the French government had entertained ways of privatizing its communications behemoth, France Télécom's unions staged massive strikes, forcing the government to retreat.[2] The acrimony between the management and unions of France Télécom led to the departure of the CEO, Marcel Roulet, at the end of August 1995.[3] Roulet's replacement, Francois Henrot, resigned after just five days. France Télécom's board hastily yet grudgingly gave its blessing to the French cabinet, which appointed Michel Bon to head the communications giant on September 13, 1995.[4]

Bon had his work cut out for him. France Télécom was some $16 billion in debt, and 95 percent of its employees were civil servants, meaning that they could not be fired. To demonstrate their sentiments and their power, the unions went on strike within weeks of Bon's arrival. The message: "Don't even think about privatizing."[5] Bon, however, was unflappable. Tall, courteous, and smooth talking, Bon had a disarming smile. Despite a dapper appearance in his impeccable suits, Bon was not flashy. He did not take the job for the money, accepting only €279,000—the lowest chief executive's salary of any blue-chip French firm.[6] Bon had exceptional French establishment credentials: training at the elite Ecole Nationale d'Administration; many years as chief executive of Europe's biggest retailer, Carrefour; and, most recently as head of France's national unemployment agency. Bon was voted manager of the year on three separate occasions while CEO of Carrefour, but was ousted from his position because of disagreements over strategy (despite boosting Carrefour's profits by 400 percent).[7]

Bon's style proved effective at calming France Télécom's unions and getting the firm ready for an initial public offering. Former France Télécom board member Elie Cohen observed of Bon, "It was a poisoned dossier before he arrived. He managed the negotiations adroitly."[8]

Bon guided France Télécom to a successful stock market listing in 1997. More than four million people bought shares, although the French government still held greater than 50 percent of the stock.[9]

Even though the French government maintained a controlling stake in France Télécom, psychologically Bon cut the cord. But he demonstrated the severance symbolically as well. When *Le Nouvel Observateur* magazine organized a group portrait of the CEOs of France's seven major government-controlled companies, Bon refused to pose; he was the only CEO to do so.[10]

Bon immediately set out to reengineer the company to "place the customer at the heart of group strategy."[11] A key part of the strategy was to become a global powerhouse, able to offer its customers virtually all telecommunications solutions. This was no small issue. France Télécom had built the first digital telecommunications network in Europe, but it was paradoxically slow to offer some of the most basic services (such as caller identification and call forwarding). Furthermore, it was way behind in Internet-based services. Recognizing the appeal of these missing services to customers (sure to be offered by upstart competitors), Bon began a crusade to introduce them.

Convinced that size and spectrum of offerings mattered in the ability to meet customers' evolving telecommunications needs, Bon led France Télécom on a voracious acquisitions binge. Bon stated, "We have the ambition to be one of the largest [telecoms] in Europe."[12]

The company purchased wireless operator Orange, Internet service provider Freeserve, and data-network company Equant. In addition, billions of dollars were spent to build next-generation mobile telephone networks. The total cost of these investments was a staggering $50 billion. Noted Bon, "It [cost] an amazing amount of money, but we have achieved what will essentially be our profile in the years to come."[13]

Bon's strategy reflected his belief that customers would begin to demand a one-stop shop. To lock in their loyalty, France Télécom had to expand its offerings. Moreover, as France Télécom's financial press releases indicated, customer loyalty had become a critical financial metric: "The customer loyalty programs introduced in 1998 in order to reduce the churn rate have been stepped up in 1999. As a result, churn has dropped to 22.6 percent in 1999, compared to 24.1 percent in 1998."[14]

The public was enamored with Bon's strategy. *CNNfn* proclaimed, "France Télécom's chairman has rebuilt the status of the company on a *global stage*."[15] By March 2000, France Télécom had grown to be France's largest company.[16]

Unfortunately, the joy was short-lived. By the end of 2001, France Télécom announced a loss of over €8 billion. The first-half results for 2002 looked much worse; the company was facing a larger loss for the first half of 2002 than for all of 2001.[17] The result was a massive slide in its stock price. From its height in March 2000 to June 2002, market capitalization dropped by 95 percent!

France Télécom's buying spree, once acclaimed as visionary, now became the butt of jokes. *Fortune* magazine lampooned France Télécom's debt as "nearly as much debt as Qwest ($25 billion), Sprint ($23 billion), and WorldCom ($30 billion) combined."[18] *Business Week* heralded "France Inc. Follies."[19] At almost $70 billion (€69 billion), however, it was an easy target. It ranked as the highest corporate debt in the world.[20]

Despite calls for his head, Bon remained committed to the fundamental correctness of his vision. "Our debt, it is not debt for nothing," argued France Télécom spokesperson Bruno Janet. "It is debt to build France Télécom as a leader in European telecommunications. Now we are number two in wireless, number two in Internet, and number one in data."[21]

In June 2002, Bon reflected, "The time of the speculators is much shorter than that of France Télécom. We wait. We are patient." He did not see his job as vulnerable unless "someone lost their nerves."[22]

Unfortunately, as France Télécom posted a €12.2 billion first-half loss on September 12, 2002, Michel Bon submitted his resignation—a full seven years after being awarded the position.[23] *Time* magazine reflected on Bon's tenure: "Michel Bon turned France Télécom from a national fixed-line phone company into a European powerhouse. But the acquisition binge that bought the company Orange, a 28.5 percent stake in MobilCom and a disastrously expensive 3G presence also left it with a staggering debt of nearly €70 billion, and as Bon resigned last week that looked like his lasting legacy."[24] France Télécom ultimately posted a loss of over €20 billion in 2002!

Turnaround specialist, manager extraordinaire, and science fiction writer Thierry Breton was chosen to replace Bon. Breton's transformation of France Télécom, returning the firm to profitability, has been rapid and astounding. As a result, *Business Week* heralded him as one of the 2004 Stars of Europe: "Creative cost-cutting and tighter financial controls let Breton boost 2003 operating income by 45 percent, to nearly $12 billion. . . . The new corporate culture at France Télécom reflects Breton's energetic personality. Gone is the paternalism that left workers feeling more comfortable than challenged. Breton also did away with weekly executive lunches. 'We're too tense for that," says the CEO [Breton], who favors sandwiches at his desk.'"[25]

Breton's transformation of France Télécom was swift and remarkable. From the end of 2002 to the end of 2004, he cut the company's debt from €69 billion to €44 billion.[26] During that same time, France Télécom's market value more than tripled, from €18.2 billion to €57.3 billion.[27]

The dramatic turn of events at France Télécom resulted in Jacques Chirac, France's president, to twice ask Breton to become his Finance Minister. After the second request (initially he wished to remain with France Télécom), Breton accepted.[28]

As a result, Breton was succeeded by Didier Lombard, who began his career at France Télécom and served as general director of industrial strategy at the Ministry of Industry. Noted Lombard, "[Thierry Breton] formulated a clear vision that will shape the group's strategy and development for several years to come."[29]

The Moral of Paying Too Much for Customer Loyalty

The saga of France Télécom under Michel Bon is unfortunate; Bon is a gifted individual who aggressively pursued a strategy that he believed would simultaneously benefit all stakeholders—customers, employees, and shareholders. Bon's failure no doubt fuels arguments against the value of pursuing customer loyalty.

There were several reasons for the failure of Bon's particular pursuit of customer loyalty; there certainly were market factors that played a role in the failure of his strategy. But there were also fundamental flaws in Bon's reasoning. These flaws insinuated themselves from some of the basic myths about customer loyalty. Chief among these was the

Source: Cartoonybin.com. Reproduced with permission.

core belief that enhancing customer loyalty always leads to profitability. While that might be true, it is never as straightforward a progression as Bon may have hoped. Another incorrect core belief was that a simple broadening of the offering would lead to greater customer loyalty. This common error relates to viewing the situation at the macroeconomic level (the global offer), instead of from a microeconomic view that would more easily foster an understanding and prediction of individual behaviors from customers. As France Télécom discovered in the quest to enhance customers' experiences (and thereby engender their loyalty), it is possible to make disastrous loyalty investment decisions.

In this chapter, we expose some of the most prevalent myths regarding customers' spending, their profitability, and its relationship to customer loyalty. By identifying certain practices as a search for fool's gold, we can concentrate on digging where the loyalty gold really is.

LOYALTY MYTH 37: Long-Term Customers Purchase More

The idea that long-term customers purchase more is a core tenet of the customer retention movement. The notion is that, like a fine cabernet, customers improve with age. Frederick Reichheld marked this idea in executives' minds indelibly: "Across a wide range of businesses, customers generate increasing profits each year they stay with a company. Why? Return customers tend to buy more from a company over time."[30]

This myth should be examined from two perspectives. One deals with the purchasing power of individual consumers over their temporal lifetimes. The other is a share-of-requirements explanation, which plays particularly well within an industrial, B2B context. (Share-of-requirements, share-of-spending, and share-of-wallet are all measures of the share of a customer's spending that a particular brand or marketer receives.)

The myth seductively dovetails with our basic understanding of the economics of individuals: Earnings generally increase with age (until retirement, at least). Therefore, it would appear to make perfect sense that because wealth tends to increase with age, customers should buy more from a company over time.

Looking purely at individual economics with regard to this myth, however, consumption is probably a more important variable to examine. Although consumption of all goods and services does tend to increase with age, it does so at a much less steep increase than that of earnings, as shown in Figure 5.1. And consumption is dispersed throughout all products and services purchased. Therefore, at the microlevel, it is highly unlikely that consumers purchase more of a product or service over time. Most of us return regularly to our grocery stores, our telephone companies, our Internet service providers, our shoe stores, and so on. Did we buy *more* food, telephone time, ISP services, or shoes simply because we returned? Obviously not. Need is the driving factor and controls our rate of consumption. There are many business sectors where this myth is nonsense.

FIGURE 5.1 Life Cycle of Earnings and Consumption

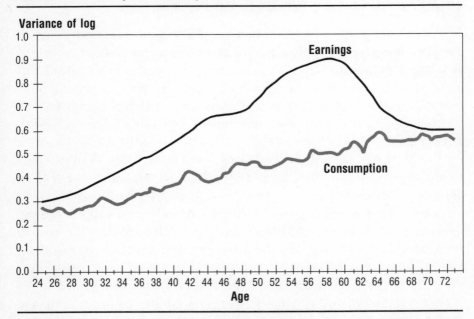

Source: Peter Rupert and Chris Telmer, "Life-cycle Income and Consumption Variability," *Economic Commentary*, Federal Reserve Bank of Cleveland (Ohio), March 1, 2001, http://www.clevelandfed.org/research/Com2001/0301rupert.htm.

On the industrial side, one can conjure the image of the salesman and purchasing agent becoming more comfortable in their interactions. As was illustrated in the Introduction, however, even in such business situations the myth is easily disproved. Reinartz and Kumar pointed out in a *Journal of Marketing* article the fallacy of this reasoning with examples from four industries.[31] The apparent relationship between customer longevity and purchase volume is correlation without causation. For most businesses, a simple point-in-time analysis of all customers would reveal that desired customers (that is, those that are profitable) would generally be customers with longer tenures with a company. But, as we explained in the Introduction, the longer tenure of desired customers could be explained primarily because their counterparts, costly customers, are more likely to frequently switch vendors, thereby shortening their tenure. Therefore, the apparent higher value of customers with longer tenures (desired customers) is really an artifact. Desired customers were spending more from the beginning—their desirability did not improve over time.

LOYALTY MYTH 38: Long-Term Customers Are More Desirable than Short-Term Customers

It is a natural extension of the underlying logic in Myth 37 that, if long-term customers are more desirable than short-term customers because they are believed to purchase more, then long-term customers must be better for business than short-term customers. Given that the foundation of this myth is incorrect, it should not be a surprise that this extension is also false.

Reinartz and Kumar's exploration referred to in Myth 37 and reported in the *Harvard Business Review* found that both long-term and short-term customer groupings were composed of subsegments of desirable and undesirable customers.[32] This is not hard to understand. Imagine being CEO of Home Depot in the United States, or CEO of Homebase in the UK (Home Depot and Homebase are do-it-yourself home improvement retailers). Who is most likely to be a desirable customer for your store: a recent purchaser of a new home or a long-time customer of your store? Likewise, it is difficult to imagine retailer

Babies "R" Us successfully nurturing highly profitable 20-year relationships, given that its products target expectant parents and parents
of children two years of age and younger. The tremendous growth
rate of this U.S. retailer proves that these short-term customers are
good customers indeed.

The problem with this myth is not just that it is wrong, but that it
disadvantages strategic decision-making by managers worldwide.
Short-term customers may be every bit as important to a firm's success
as long-term customers, and sometimes they are the core of a company's current business.

LOYALTY MYTH 39: Share-of-Wallet Increases as Customer Lifetimes Increase

The belief that loyal customers increase their share-of-wallet as their
customer lifetime lengthens also flows from Myth 37; if long-term customers purchase more, then it must be because they are consolidating
purchases with a single provider. Given that most managers would define customer loyalty as manifest in the consolidation of purchases
with a favored brand or company, this myth seems completely logical.

Without question, loyal customers do allocate a higher share of
their spending with a given company than with its competitors. The
problem is the idea that customers allocate greater percentages of
their spending with a company over time. Nonsense! Why would a
loyal customer consistently increase share over time? She is already
loyal; therefore, she already allocates a high share of her spending
with the firm. Does her loyalty grow even stronger over time, resulting
in an ever increasing share of spending? This is what the myth implies.

The reality is that in many categories, time acts as a detriment to
the allocation of spending. Take financial services as an example. As
earnings increase, so too do an individual's investment needs. As a result, individuals often find themselves allocating smaller percentages
of their investable assets with a particular product or firm as they age,
even while they may be increasing their absolute dollar amount invested (because of increased earnings and disposable income) with
the product or firm.

LOYALTY MYTH 40: Increasing Customer Share-of-Wallet Is Driven by Increasing Customer Loyalty

Increases in customer loyalty will parallel increases in customers' share-of-wallet. But it is wrong to presume that share-of-wallet increases are driven by increases in customer loyalty. A number of issues affect customers' spending allocation.

Increased loyalty is not typically the reason for increased share-of-spending; price is. Managers can increase customers' share-of-spending by dropping their price. Brand managers are universally aware of the effect of price promotions on sales: typically, large spikes in sales volume. Customers typically load up on the discounted brand, in effect warehousing the product for future use.

As a result, share-of-wallet does increase, but the emotional aspects of loyalty have been damaged. Customers are taught that their preferred brands are worth less than they imagined they were. Sales levels in the future, at the original price, will be harder to maintain.

Source: Cartoonybin.com. Reproduced with permission.

LOYALTY MYTH 41: Spending on Customer Service Increases Customer Loyalty

Not necessarily. Spending on customer service can mean many different things. Often spending to improve service quality results in no appreciable benefit. Before any spending is committed on service quality in an effort to enhance customer loyalty, the relationship between the proposed enhancement and customer loyalty must be established. Then the projected financial impact of the effort should be calculated. If the effort is not likely to produce a positive return on investment, then it probably is not significantly enhancing customer loyalty. Additionally, for many customer segments, spending to improve customer service will have no impact on customer loyalty. Some customers are driven by price, location, or other factors.

Source: Cartoonybin.com. Reproduced with permission.

For many business categories, service is not the driver of customer loyalty—product function is. Think of the loyal Coca-Cola customer. Loyal Coke drinkers may associate many positive emotional experiences with the brand, though they seldom relate to the service experience they receive from the Coca-Cola company. Still, it would be difficult to argue that the brand does not have an extremely loyal customer base.

LOYALTY MYTH 42: Loyal Customers Are Less Price Sensitive

One of the proposed virtues of customer loyalty is that "[loyal customers] will often pay a premium to continue to do business with you rather than switch to a competitor with whom they are neither familiar nor comfortable."[33] There are probably limited examples where this is true, but certainly not "often," unless liberally tempered with the qualifier, "a competitor with whom they are neither familiar nor comfortable." Loyal customers tend to be more price sensitive. Although they might not switch to an unfamiliar or uncomfortable competitor, it is unlikely that a category would lack a competitor with whom customers were familiar and comfortable given the proclivity of brand polygamy we have previously discussed. Most customers have somewhere else to go.

In their research, Reinartz and Kumar did not find that loyal customers were paying a higher price from a preferred supplier for the same bundle of goods offered elsewhere for less. In one business-to-business example, they found that long-term customers consistently paid 5 percent and 7 percent less than did new customers.[34] The same thing applies to retail customers as well. An article in the *Washington Post* noted, "In a subtle shift of marketing tactics, some retailers have stepped up coupon offers directed at their most loyal customers in a bid to attract repeat visits from big spenders. . . . Eager to wean themselves from discounts for the masses, retailers hope more targeted coupons will limit big bargains to a pool of their best customers."[35] In other words, loyal customers may often pay lower prices, but are unlikely to pay higher prices.

LOYALTY MYTH 43: Loyal Customers Are Less Expensive to Service than Nonloyal Customers

The fallacy that loyal customers are less expensive to service than nonloyal customers has its origins in the manufacturing environment. At its foundation are two seminal findings that dramatically influenced the strategy and tactics of manufacturers around the world. The first is commonly referred to as the experience curve (also called the learning curve), originally popularized by the Boston Consulting Group. Figure 5.2 depicts this curve.

In essence, the theory behind the experience curve states that the costs of complex products and services will decline approximately 20 to 30 percent with each doubling of accumulated experience.[36] Experience curve strategies have been integrated into the strategies of companies since the 1960s.

The other source of this myth rests in the quality movement of the 1980s and 1990s. Manufacturers found that improving quality produced greater cost savings than the costs of improving operations. In essence, improved quality created operating efficiencies that lowered manufacturing costs.[37]

FIGURE 5.2   The Experience Curve

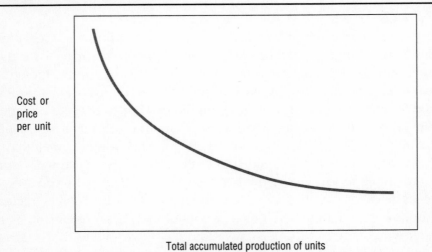

Total accumulated production of units

Both the experience curve and the operating efficiencies of quality have consistently proven true in the manufacturing environment. As a result, it would appear intuitive that they should likewise hold true in the service environment. It is important to remember that the customer retention and customer loyalty movement—initially, at least—revolved around services, which is why Reichheld and Sasser's seminal *Harvard Business Review* article (referred to in the Introduction) was entitled "Zero Defections: Quality Comes to Services."

Reichheld argues that customer loyalty translates into cost savings for companies, stating that "your operating costs to serve them [loyal customers] decline" over time.[38] The reason: "As the company gains experience with its customers, it can serve them more efficiently."[39] Given the results that manufacturers experienced through learning efficiencies and quality improvement, Reichheld's assertions sound not only plausible but probable.

But the separation between appearing probable and occurring is all too often a chasm. In none of the companies Reinartz and Kumar tracked were loyal customers consistently less expensive to manage than short-term customers. The only correlation they could find was in the high-tech service sector, and here loyal customers were more expensive to serve.[40]

While a company may know more about its loyal customers, loyal customers know the firm better as well. As a result, they may be more demanding of the company through better knowledge of the inner workings of the system. This allows them to seek recourse for what they believe to be inadequate treatment, and they are more likely to get perks from the relationship, which cost money to administer and fulfill.

We end discussion of this myth with a statement made by a senior officer of a large airline when he was presenting to officers of the firm. In particular, he was discussing the complaints of flight attendants regarding the airline's high-mileage frequent-flier customers. He noted that the crew complained of these passengers being difficult and demanding. His reply: "Yes, but they're *ours.*"

LOYALTY MYTH 44: Loyal Customers Are More Profitable; Loyal Customers Are Always Profitable Customers

Loyalty does not equal profitability. For many companies, the majority of customers who would be considered both attitudinally and behaviorally loyal would not be profitable. That is because, as was pointed out in the Introduction, customers tend to fall into one of three broad groups: Desired (profitable), Break-even, or Costly (unprofitable). For most firms, the most profitable 20 percent of customers generate between 150 and 300 percent of total profits; the middle 60 to 70 percent of customers about break even; and the least profitable 10 to 20 percent of customers lose 50 to 200 percent of the firm's total profits. That means that 80 percent of a firm's customers do not provide an acceptable rate of return.

Unfortunately, loyal customers exist within each segment. And,

Source: Cartoonybin.com. Reproduced with permission.

all too frequently, this means that the majority of loyal customers do not produce an acceptable rate of return.

LOYALTY MYTH 45: Customer Satisfaction Brings Customer Loyalty

Without a doubt, customer satisfaction and customer loyalty are linked. But the linkage is not straightforward and it isn't linear. Clearly, dissatisfied customers are more likely to defect than are satisfied customers. The problem with the customer satisfaction–customer loyalty link, however, is that most firms do not have a sufficient groundswell of dissatisfied customers to make them notice the severe impact of dissatisfaction. If they did, they would not be in business for long.

Most companies have customers who are moderately satisfied. For almost all business enterprises worldwide, greater than 85 percent of their customers would be classified as satisfied. As a result, satisfaction (the absence of dissatisfaction) is typically not a point of competitive differentiation.

With regard to the relationship between satisfaction and loyalty, we need to think of satisfaction as falling into one of three general categories: dissatisfied, merely satisfied, and delighted. It is not until customers achieve this upper level of satisfaction, delight, that satisfaction meaningfully influences customer loyalty. (See Figure 5.3.)

Even when satisfaction reaches delight levels, however, it is important to remember that several additional factors influence customers' levels of loyalty:

- Costs of switching (time, money, effort, etc.).
- A strong predisposition to switch service providers or brands (i.e., some customers enjoy variety seeking).
- Competitive actions (for example, discounts, coupons, promotions).

FIGURE 5.3 Delight Curve

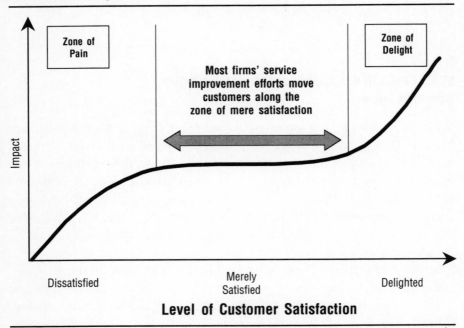

Source: Adapted from Roland T. Rust, Anthony J. Zahorik, and Timothy L. Keiningham, *Return on Quality: Measuring the Financial Impact of Your Company's Quest for Quality* (New York: Irwin Professional Publishing, 1994).

While customer delight may be a necessary requirement for customer loyalty, it does not guarantee customer loyalty.

LOYALTY MYTH 46: Customer Revenue Is a Good Predictor of Profitability

Most firms treat customer revenue and customer profitability as synonymous. Revenue is a measure of purchase volume and, therefore, correlated to customer loyalty. As a result, firms tend to expend a great deal of effort on their highest-revenue customers. But revenue is typically not a good predictor of profitability. Some of the largest

Source: Cartoonybin.com. Reproduced with permission.

customers are the most unprofitable. As Professors Kaplan and Narayanan of the Harvard Business School observe: "A company cannot lose large amounts of money with small customers. It doesn't do enough business with a small customer to incur large (absolute) losses. Only a large customer, working in a particularly perverse way, can be a large loss customer. Large customers tend to be either the most profitable or the least profitable in the entire customer base. It is unusual for a large customer to be in the middle of the total profitability rankings."[41]

There is no substitute for knowing the profitability of customers. Chasing revenue may expand market share, which is sometimes a valid strategy, as Apple discovered in its early battles with Microsoft, but it is definitely not a profit maximizing strategy—at least in the near term.

Source: Cartoonybin.com. Reproduced with permission.

LOYALTY MYTH 47: Customer Loyalty Is Easy to Measure

There is no universally agreed-upon definition of loyalty. Instead, there are three popular underlying theories of customer loyalty, summarized here:

1. Loyalty is expressed as an attitudinal commitment that leads to a relationship with a brand.
2. Loyalty is defined as a pattern of repeat purchases.
3. Loyalty is a combination of attitude and behavior moderated by a customer's individual characteristics, circumstances, and/or the purchase situation.[42]

Our own definition of customer loyalty is discussed in Chapter 7. Since there is no consensus on what loyalty is, there is no easy measurement system, although several have been proposed. And, as we are about to discover in our next debunked myth, industry and sector influence what is meant by customer loyalty.

Because loyalty enjoys many varied definitions and likely is influenced by many factors, the lack of any universal measure is understandable. How pundits could claim its easy measurement and not be challenged is unclear. Operationally, many firms have defaulted to the use of attitudinal measures to potentially identify loyal customers. A common approach is to use a combination of three questions claimed to identify loyal or secure customers. The three questions measure:

1. Overall satisfaction with the brand.
2. Likelihood of repurchasing the brand.
3. Willingness to recommend the brand to others.

Customers exhibiting "top-box" scores on all three of these measures are considered loyal customers. Though used frequently, there are no published, empirical proofs of this system, especially relating scores to actual purchase behavior. And, note that the system is not only totally attitudinal but as administered in one questionnaire or interview is likely highly intercorrelated.

LOYALTY MYTH 48: The Concept of Loyalty Is the Same Across Industries and Sectors

Perusing some of the more than 40,000 books espousing customer loyalty as an appropriate business strategy, one would conclude that most firms operate in a high-involvement, high personal identity category similar to that of Harley Davidson. Such companies do exist, but the number of categories where people would consider tattooing a brand name onto their arm is quite small. Loyalty to a toothpaste brand is unlikely to result in customers becoming walking billboards.

The degree of customers' loyalty is strongly mitigated by the category in which a product competes. Attitudinal and relationship approaches to loyalty work, although they are not universally applicable. They work particularly well when customers are making high-risk or important decisions. Relationship approaches do not work particularly well, however, with low-risk, frequently purchased brands. And they rarely work when customers buy the product on impulse or as a means of seeking variety. These scenarios represent a substantial number of product categories.

Research shows that only a few brands have earned relationship status with their customers. A 2001 study of more than 40 brands in seven major categories found that only 35 percent of customers claimed to have a solid, growing relationship with any of the brands studied.[43] So for all of the talk about customer relationship management, customers have not been overly impressed. Given the difference in the concept of loyalty across categories, it is easy to understand why.

SETTING THE RECORD STRAIGHT: LOYALTY'S RELATIONSHIP WITH SHARE OF BUSINESS AND PROFITS

Michel Bon thought he knew what France Télécom's customers wanted. He threw tremendous amounts of capital at acquiring those allied services. He failed, however, to conduct an appropriate ROI analysis; he built it, but they did not stay (or come) in numbers sufficient to offset his vast investments.

Virtually everything we have been told about the relationship between customer loyalty and financial outcomes is bunk. As we pointed out in the Introduction, "The difficult truth regarding customer loyalty is that how it links to growth and profitability is far more complex than we have been led to believe. A blind pursuit of customer loyalty is at best a case of misallocated resources. But at worst it is a recipe for financial disaster."

That is not to suggest that fostering customer loyalty cannot be a profitable strategy; indeed, loyalty can be a highly profitable means of differentiating a firm from its competitors. But profits are not the foregone conclusion that the myths surrounding loyalty falsely suggest.

> **Loyalty Truth 5:** The chain of events from loyalty to profits is twisted and complex. Learn the specific response patterns of your customers and your industry.

Know your customers and their response functions before you invest in loyalty. There are no surrogates for understanding how your own customers will behave. The chain from loyalty to profitability is not straight; to make it work for you requires an understanding of your unique customers and situation. Relying on simple, conventional wisdom can lead to financial disaster.

The justification for any business to pursue a customer loyalty strategy is its connection to the bottom line; otherwise, the effort is unsustainable. Fortunately, the ability to achieve this objective is more than a faint hope. Before we conclude this book, we will point the way.

CHAPTER 6

Loyalty Myths
Regarding Employees

Source: Cartoonybin.com. Reproduced with permission.

Smile, though your heart is aching . . .
—"Smile," by Turner, Parsons,
and Chaplin

The lyrics to the song "Smile" were an afterthought to a musical score Charlie Chaplin had composed for his film *Modern Times,* one of the last silent films. The movie followed Chaplin's Little Tramp character as he struggled to survive in an increasingly industrialized world. With the lyrics added, "Smile" enjoyed considerable popularity long after memories of the movie had faded. The song serves as a serenade to downtrodden and heartbroken individuals.

THE PARABLE OF THE MANDATED SMILE

Considering the song's lyrics, "Smile" would have been an appropriate anthem for employees of the Safeway grocery chain in the late 1990s. Safeway, the second largest grocery store chain in the United States, was well known for treating its customers with personalized attention and friendly service. Its reputation for friendly service was no accident—it was mandated. Safeway's management was determined to make the chain number one in its industry for customer service. So management required all 150,000 employees to be friendly.

In 1993, Safeway began phasing in an even more aggressive friendliness campaign under its Superior Service program. In this expanded program, employees were expected to display certain behaviors. They were told they should anticipate customers' needs, make selling suggestions, thank customers by name, and offer to carry out their groceries. They were also told they were expected to smile and make eye contact with Safeway customers.

Smile! Or You're Fired

In January 1998, Safeway escalated its enforcement of the Superior Service policy, using undercover shoppers, called "mystery shoppers,"

154

to assess compliance with the program by individual employees in each of its stores. The mystery shoppers were average people hired to pose as customers and sent into stores to score how well each employee was carrying out the policy's required service elements. The mystery shoppers observed specific employee behaviors, noting if the employee (1) made initial eye contact and greeted the shopper sincerely with a smile; (2) anticipated a need and voluntarily offered assistance; and (3) used the shopper's last name if and when the opportunity was presented. Reports of the "mystery shops" were posted in store break rooms.

Less-than-satisfactory performance by an employee led to remedial training, disciplinary letters, and, ultimately, termination. Employees who failed to get a perfect score on three out of five undercover shopping reports were sent to a special eight-hour training program that offered them advice on how to do a better job. (The program came to be referred to by employees as the "smile school.") If sales clerks failed to post acceptable scores on subsequent mystery shops after taking the course, they were sent back for more training. Any employee making more than three visits to "smile school" could be fired.[1] As Larree Renda, a senior vice president at Safeway, noted, "I think our service is a big deal. Our customers deserve to be treated with courtesy. . . . It's part of our definition of service, what it takes to provide a high level of service to our customers."[2]

Appropriate Goal, Questionable Execution

The idea that customer service should be a requirement for retail employees sounds like a no-brainer. Friendliness is obviously good business. Who could reasonably argue with a policy designed to ensure that customers received superior service? Unfortunately, sometimes things that seem so very right can go very wrong.

For many Safeway employees, requiring them to smile at *every* customer was no laughing matter. In retrospect it appears that some customers mistakenly interpreted the displayed friendliness as flirting. This was particularly true in interactions between male customers and female employees. Apparently some men wishfully mistook a female Safeway employee's friendliness for a come-on. Employees were quick to report that the smile-and-make-eye-contact rule was leading to a higher number of sexual harassment incidents committed by customers.

Employees began filing grievances with their union; they also filed charges of discrimination with the Equal Employment Opportunity Commission (EEOC) and the California Department of Fair Employment and Housing. In turn, the employees' union filed charges with the National Labor Relations Board. Ironically, employees charged that the company had fostered a "hostile work environment" by forcing smiles. Matthew Ross, an attorney for the union representing Safeway employees explained, "There's nothing wrong with asking food clerks to be courteous to customers. If you can't put the customer first, you really shouldn't work in the retail or food industry. What gets objectionable is when they take away the discretion of the clerks to control how they interact with customers."[3]

Richelle Roberts, a Safeway employee who filed charges with the EEOC, concurred: "We have no quarrel with the idea of providing our customers with excellent service. The company is right to stress service. But the company goes too far when it makes smiling at work a rule and attempts to regulate precisely how we interact with customers."[4] Added Amy Kinyon, another employee who filed charges, "By rigidly enforcing these kinds of requirements, especially with the use of mystery shoppers, the company is forcing us to suspend our natural self-defense mechanism of avoiding contact with men who act inappropriately towards us."[5]

The Moral of the Mandated Smile

The Superior Service program was a boon for Safeway's business. The company achieved some of the most spectacular financial returns in its industry throughout most of the 1990s. As reporter Bill Ritter of ABC-TV's *20-20* news program noted, "This friendly policy has meant a big improvement for Safeway. Sales and profits are way up. Customer complaints are way down. In fact, everything seems perfect, except for that sex thing."[6]

Although Safeway's Superior Service program made customers

happier and enriched the company's bottom line, it was far from a success among employees. As one reporter noted, "Safeway Inc. either is in denial about a serious employee morale problem, or its . . . stores are staffed by a handful of misanthropes and slackers who can't stand the notion of grinning widely as they go the extra yard to please the supermarket chain's customers."[7] Either way, employee satisfaction and customer satisfaction were moving in opposite directions, as were employee satisfaction and the company's financial performance. Safeway discovered the downside of low employee morale during a long-lasting strike that was financially devastating to the firm and resulted in net losses for fiscal years 2002 and 2003.

Unfortunately, Safeway's example is far from atypical. All too often businesses manipulate their employees and their employees' behavior in the pursuit of customer loyalty. But mandating customer-friendly behaviors is not the same thing as instilling customer friendliness in

Source: Cartoonybin.com. Reproduced with permission.

employees. Worse still, as Safeway discovered, it can actually erode employees' desire to interact with customers.

Five common loyalty myths underlie most of these often-misdirected initiatives. Each myth seems intuitively correct and therefore alluring. They are myths nonetheless.

LOYALTY MYTH 49: Employee Satisfaction and Customer Loyalty Go Hand-in-Hand

The management perspective is simple: Happy employees help create happy customers. Employees who service happy customers are more likely to emerge from the interaction happy . . . And so on and on the interaction spirals, virtually feeding on itself. This effect has been popularized in the concept of the "satisfaction mirror" (i.e., employee satisfaction leads to customer satisfaction and business results), first described in an article in the *Harvard Business Review*.[8] The article, written by a number of highly respected Harvard professors, established a theory of linkage between the level of service provided by businesses and their profitability. It served as an impetus for a reexamination of how employees were treated within their workplaces. The argument was largely intuitive, stimulating others to explore it more scientifically.

Virtually all of the studies that tested the satisfaction mirror concept have identified some linkage between employee satisfaction and customer satisfaction, between employee satisfaction and customer loyalty, or both. The discovered linkages, however, have ranged from negative to positive, and a few studies yielded no correlation at all. The necessary conclusion? Employee satisfaction does not universally nor unambiguously create customer loyalty.

The lack of a consistent, positive linkage supporting this myth should not be taken as an invitation to abuse employees or treat them with indifference. Although there may not be a direct relationship between employee satisfaction and customer loyalty, pervasive and continuing low employee morale will exact an ultimate toll. Unhappy employees can hurt operations in a myriad of ways: absenteeism, low productivity, uncooperative spirit, filing complaints, supporting strikes, and so forth. And as former Customer Satisfaction Director of AT&T, Ray Kordupleski, noted, "I have found that no one [employee] in any organization can totally satisfy a customer. But any one [employee] *can* totally dissatisfy a customer."[9]

While employee satisfaction isn't the boon promised to businesses, employee dissatisfaction has led to disastrous results for many firms, as Safeway discovered.

LOYALTY MYTH 50: Employee Satisfaction Leads to Business Results

The belief that employee satisfaction is important to business outcomes has been around for ages, as far back as the seventeenth century, when an Italian named Bernardino Ramazzini reported on the feelings of workers who dug and maintained cesspools. There are probably a subsequent 7,000 or more identifiable investigations on the subject. Unfortunately, culling through the findings of these studies looking for relationships between employee morale and standard measures of productivity finds a mixed bag: positive correlations, negative correlations, and, in some situations, no correlations whatsoever.[10]

Similarly studies specifically testing the association between employee satisfaction and business results typically discover some linkage. Just as was the case with examinations of employee satisfaction and customer satisfaction, they have failed to reveal consistent indications. Some correlate negatively, some positively, and a few fail to show any correlation.

Most investigations into the linkage between employee satisfaction and customer satisfaction and, ultimately, corporate profits have tended to study absolute levels of employee measures (e.g., a rating of 7.3 on a 10-point scale). The authors were fortunate to have access to data sets from several firms (both U.S. and European). In exploring the nature of the linkage between employee measures and business outcomes within these data sets we made a surprising discovery: The *consistency* of employee feelings was more important than the absolute level in building a cause-effect model!

Employees, like customers, appear to establish thresholds of expected performance. That is, they will accustom themselves to less than ideal circumstances so long as those conditions don't worsen. In Chapter 5, Myth 44, we saw how customers adopt thresholds of performance. Employees similarly acclimate to thresholds of environment, even though they may be less than perfect. If, however, these thresholds are breached by deteriorating conditions (breaking through a minimally acceptable level), then there are repercussions in employees' performance, and customer feelings and profits are likely to suffer. But if employee attitudes remain constant or advance slowly, without receding, then customer attitudes and profits are more likely to improve.[11] Again, in our data, the linkage to business outcomes was not universal. Unfortunately, firms with satisfied employees can still find themselves losing out to competitors and ultimately going out of business.

Source: Cartoonybin.com. Reproduced with permission.

LOYALTY MYTH 51: Loyal Employees Create Loyal Customers

Employee satisfaction has not always been shown to link directly to customer loyalty, so a new myth has evolved with a slightly different target. The amended myth holds that it is not employee satisfaction but employee *loyalty* that results in customer loyalty. Clearly, this statement also seems intuitively correct. Belief in this myth is further fueled by occasional examples in the business and popular press that offer support for this argument.

For example, in a survey of more than 7,500 workers, more than half considered themselves committed to their employers. Shareholders investing in the companies with committed employees received, on average, a 112 percent return on their investment over three years. Investment in companies where employees considered themselves average or below average in commitment to the firm returned an average of only 76 percent.[12]

Because of its assumed impact on corporate performance, for the past 30 years, employee commitment has been one of the most popular research areas in the fields of industrial psychology and organizational behavior. However, paradoxical as it might seem, researchers in these disciplines have been unable to confirm a relationship between employee commitment and business performance.[13] Just as with employee satisfaction research, some studies have been able to show a relationship, while other studies have been unable to establish any. One team of researchers noted, "Although higher levels of commitment may relate to improved job performance in some situations . . . the present findings suggest that commitment has very little direct influence on performance in most instances."[14]

The Service Management faculty at the Harvard Business School suggests that the strength of the relationship may be contingent upon four elements describing employee performance: capability, satisfaction, loyalty, and productivity.[15] These four elements are thought to directly influence customer satisfaction (and ultimately loyalty) in the following manner:

1. Capability: Capable employees can deliver high-value service to customers. This implies that employees have the training, tools, procedures, and rules to deliver good service.

2. Satisfaction: Satisfied employees are more likely to treat customers better than are their dissatisfied counterparts.

3. Loyalty: Loyal employees are more willing to suppress short-term demands for the long-term benefit of the organization. As such, they may themselves place a priority on good customer service. Loyal employees also stay with their organizations longer, reducing the cost of turnover and its negative effect on service quality.

4. Productivity: Productive employees have the potential to raise the value of a firm's offerings to its customers. Greater productivity can lower costs of operations, which can mean lower prices for customers.

The combination of these four factors makes intuitive sense. In addition to the traditionally emphasized elements of employee satisfaction and loyalty, this perspective adds the dimensions of capability

Source: Cartoonybin.com. Reproduced with permission.

and productivity. The theory, yet to be proven, emphasizes that employee loyalty is not a singular, direct link to customer loyalty.

LOYALTY MYTH 52: Employees Are Rewarded for Increasing Customer Loyalty or Creating Loyal Customers

It was mentioned earlier that customer loyalty was one of the most important goals of worldwide CEOs, as reported in a 2002 survey conducted by the Conference Board. With CEOs' acceptance of the importance of customer loyalty, one would hope that this objective would have percolated down to employees in the workforce and have similarly become their focus as well. Unfortunately, the corporate environment seems to have interfered with employee acceptance of the objective. Despite the commitment to customer loyalty among CEOs, it is typically not part of employees' performance objectives. In fact, rarely do employees have any customer loyalty metric as part of their compensation systems. Employees are subjected to a broad list of performance objectives, and if any objective is even remotely related to customer loyalty, it will likely account for only a minuscule part of their total potential bonus. Employees with any loyalty metric typically have an aggregate customer satisfaction measure they must reach to achieve a full bonus. (The foibles of such systems are apparent when an automobile salesperson says something to the effect of, "If you'll give me a perfect rating, I'll see you get a set of matching floor mats for your car." Not exactly a pristine system.)

Most employee objectives will be oriented to tangibles: for example, total sales, shrink (the level of pilferage), staffing costs, and so forth. Managers no doubt believe that given the nature of tangible measures, they are much more within their control. Thus they tend to focus on these measures before considering any softer issues like customer loyalty. Customer metrics, even when they exist, can often be diametrically opposed to the more basic tangible measures (for example, staffing costs versus customer loyalty).

Doing things that might engender customer loyalty in the long term will frequently lose out to efforts to maximize profits (by minimizing costs) in the short term. Furthermore, the economic models of many businesses do not fund or support the development of actual customer loyalty.

The reality is that many large businesses operate at relatively low profit margins. Their economics tend to be driven by volume. For example, while a loyal customer's visits to a supermarket might provide an opportunity for the store's personnel to become acquainted with the customer, it would be virtually impossible to engage most customers in meaningful conversations. Employees that did this too frequently would have to be fired because their firms would literally shut down from inefficiencies. As writer Calvin Trillin noted on the subject, "The people have to move through the line at a certain speed or everything will go wrong."[16]

Employees simply aren't motivated to increase customer loyalty, nor to create loyal customers. And employers, because of their singular focus on near-term profits, don't generally place a priority on efforts that would help employees increase customer loyalty or create loyalty customers.

I know the costume is silly, but it's really cut down on my workload.

Source: Cartoonybin.com. Reproduced with permission.

LOYALTY MYTH 53: Empowering Employees Is the Best Way to Create Satisfied, Loyal Customers

We have already alluded to employee capabilities in Myth 51. Employee empowerment emerged from the "quality of work life" movement of the 1960s.[17] Empowerment, though not uniformly defined, generally means transferring some managerial discretion for the solution of business and customer problems to levels lower in the organization than tradition dictates. For example, at one time, employees of the Ritz-Carlton hotel chain were allowed a certain number of hotel dollars that they could use at their discretion to solve any guest problems they encountered over the course of their shift. By showing management's trust in the abilities of employees, employee empowerment is thought to make employees happier.

Employee happiness has been a prevailing theme for some. The book *First, Break All the Rules*, describes the Gallup Organization's Q12 inventory, which asks employees, among other issues, "Do [you] have a best friend at work?"[18] Having a best friend suggests enjoying oneself or possibly being happy on the job. In contrast, some have questioned what happiness has to do with employment, believing that theorists following this line of reasoning have misinterpreted the business context. The golden rule of such investigations, "Don't measure what you can't control," seems to suggest that managers would be largely unable to influence this outcome. Yet Gallup finds it to be one of its most discriminating Q12 measures.

Is employee happiness a relevant strategic goal of business organizations? We are not suggesting that organizations should not want their employees to be happy; rather, that an individual employee's happiness is not the overriding objective or concern of any for-profit enterprise. If it were, work would be play. Regardless of how much employees enjoy their jobs, most workers would do something else were they to suddenly find themselves wealthy.

Led by Professor Ben Schneider, some people in the services sector have been delivering a more realistic message: It is not how happy your employees are that helps satisfy customers and improve business results. What really matters is how well equipped your employees are for accomplishing their duties—empowerment exchanged for enablement. Schneider created the concept of service climate: an atmosphere and conditions that enhance employees' ability to properly carry out their responsibilities.[19]

Enablement generally has to do with three issues:

1. How well equipped employees are to handle their day-in, day-out responsibilities. For example, employees might be responsible for maintaining a complicated inventory but might not have computerized, wireless bar code readers. This would be an example of poor enablement.

2. How well employees understand the policies, practices, and procedures they are asked to perform and enforce. Telling frontline employees to charge customers for routine teller operations is one thing; showing them how costly the operations are to the organization, and thereby justifying the fees they are asked to collect, is another.

3. Whether employees believe that management will support the policies they have to enforce if customers question them. If employees perceive that management will overturn any directive they attempt to enforce if the customer escalates the problem, they are likely to feel like an unsupported line of defense.

SETTING THE RECORD STRAIGHT: CUSTOMER LOYALTY AND EMPLOYEE LOYALTY

Safeway had an appropriate goal: to differentiate itself from its competitors based on a promise of courteous, friendly service. In a category where competition generally focused on price, this was a unique positioning. Unfortunately, although the strategy was right, Safeway did not think through its effective implementation. Making friendliness a corporate process by mandating smiles on employees' faces was both a questionable measure and objectionable to employees in certain circumstances. In essence, the company mandated a policy that eliminated employees' discretion. The results backfired. Initially, customer satisfaction was improved and revenues grew, but it was at the expense of employee satisfaction and loyalty.

Without question, employees are critical to the creation of loyal customers, and the purpose of exposing these loyalty myths was not to suggest otherwise. We can all think of instances where the actions of employees enhanced our loyalty to a firm. The problem, however, is that the role of employees in building customer loyalty is far more complex than the myths imply. Customer loyalty can and often does grow in the absence of satisfied or loyal employees.

So the issue is not whether it is better for companies to have satisfied and loyal employees. Even if customer loyalty is independent of employee satisfaction and loyalty, there remains the positive relationship between these elements and employee retention. The cost savings in recruiting and training resulting from reduced employee turnover alone will justify striving to achieve employee satisfaction.

Loyalty Truth 6: Satisfied and loyal employees can make a difference, but customer satisfaction and loyalty can and often does happen in the absence of employee satisfaction and loyalty.

Without question, employees matter to the success of any firm. Furthermore, developing relationships with customers frequently demands a bond between employee and customer. But employee satisfaction and employee loyalty are only two of a myriad of factors that ultimately affect the loyalty of customers, and loyalty can still be had in the absence of either of them. For example, the workers who built our car, washing machine, or computer may or may not enjoy their jobs, but we could be very loyal to the brands associated with each. We as customers would not have any demonstrable evidence of employees' levels of satisfaction and loyalty unless employees' morale had reached a point that it affected the quality of the merchandise we bought.

Therefore, when thinking of the role of employees in building customer loyalty, it is necessary first to focus on customers' needs. The first step is to align processes around customer needs and to align people and resources to support these processes. This is best done using enabled employees, as we have described, in a hospitable work environment. When done properly, this yields satisfied employees who are committed and enabled to foster customer loyalty.

CHAPTER 7

The Foundations of Customer Loyalty

Source: Cartoonybin.com. Reproduced with permission.

Loyalty is dead, the experts proclaim, and the statistics seem to bear them out. On average, U.S. corporations lose half their customers in five years, half their employees in four, and half their investors in less than one. We seem to face a future in which the only business relationships will be opportunistic transactions between virtual strangers.[1]

   —Frederick F. Reichheld, Director Emeritus and Bain fellow,
   Bain & Company, Inc.

THE PARABLE OF A GENERIC WORLD

The cult classic film *Repo Man* takes a satirical look at punk sensibilities: nihilism, hedonism, and anticommercialism. *Repo Man* follows 1980s punk Otto (played by Emilio Estevez), who, in one day, loses his job at a grocery store, loses his girlfriend to his best friend, and stumbles into a new career as a repo man. The film's story takes place in a world filled with white-labeled, black-lettered generic products. People eat from cans labeled "FOOD" washed down with six-packs of "DRINK."

The generic world of *Repo Man* startles the senses because the mind immediately recognizes the inherent challenges of living in such a generic society. Even a world offering slightly more information, where the broad product label "FOOD" is further explained with additional categories (e.g., bread, meat, vegetables) or subcategories (e.g., bagels, beef, peas) would still be unmanageable for most modern-day consumers who have been raised with nationally branded products and services. Given the ambiguous productscape of the movie, even people who would ordinarily rile against big corporations would have to acknowledge finding value in the concept of branding, and would hold some degree of loyalty for different brands and companies.

The Moral of a Generic World

Stand in any grocery aisle for more than a few seconds and you will observe consumers passing over scores of competing products to extract a specific brand. Imagine Elaine, a housewife and mother of two, who perfunctorily shops for groceries in her neighborhood store every Thursday. On one such excursion, she enters the store and browses the aisles on her habitual route—making sure not to miss any item diligently jotted onto her shopping list the night before. Arriving in the condiments aisle, she reaches without hesitation and picks up a bottle of Heinz ketchup, a favorite with her nine-year-old son Brian. Elaine realizes there are other ketchup brands in this aisle, even some that are less expensive. But she disregards these differences and always selects Heinz ketchup.

Such behavior is a phenomenon that transcends Elaine's purchasing of mealtime condiments. It is behavior that most of us can easily relate to because we buy products this way all the time. Regardless of whether we are purchasing ketchup, tires, or a new pair of skis or golf clubs, we are inextricably bound to one brand over most of the others.

Source: Cartoonybin.com. Reproduced with permission.

What is the primary motive underlying this bond? Most simply stated, it is loyalty to a brand. Elaine knows what Heinz ketchup will taste like; there is no risk involved, the product will offer no surprises. She is reasonably certain she will enjoy it as a condiment for hamburgers and fries, and she knows her son will be happy to see his favorite ketchup on the table as opposed to another brand. Elaine's purchase decision is thus positively reinforced, and her future likelihood of re-purchasing Heinz ketchup increases.

WHAT EXACTLY IS LOYALTY?

While we all have an intuitive understanding of what loyalty is, based on our own loyal behavior, Professor Rich Oliver offers a reasonably comprehensive definition of loyalty:

> A deeply held commitment to rebuy or repatronize a pre-ferred product/service consistently in the future, thereby causing repetitive same-brand or same brand-set purchasing despite situational influences and marketing efforts having the potential to cause switching behavior.[2]

Loyalty is, in simpler terms, a reliance on a particular brand or company even though numerous satisfactory alternatives may exist. This means foregoing the pleasure (or agony) of experimenting with other brands. It also means paying whatever price the brand to which one is loyal is currently selling for, without reappraising the compara-tive value of the purchase. In short, the brand to which one is loyal enjoys an enviable position; it is not in a horse race with other brands, nor does it have to be competitively priced. It is in its own, secure world.

No wonder customer loyalty is coveted by businesses. They crave the success and the value that loyalty-bound customers can bring to their enterprise.

The history of exploration into customer loyalty has been long, if not enlightening. Melvin Copeland, a sociologist, was one of the first to speak of customer loyalty from a theoretical perspective. In 1923 he advanced the concept of *customer insistence.*[3] Jacoby and Chestnut provide an excellent review of the subsequent evolution of thinking, identifying as many as 53 alternative operational definitions of loyalty![4] However numerous, these 53 definitions can be economically categorized under three basic approaches that have evolved to conceptualize loyalty: a behavioral (purchasing) approach, an attitudinal (feelings) approach, and a hybrid approach incorporating consumer characteristics and purchase situation specifics (circumstances). These are summarized in Figure 7.1.

FIGURE 7.1 Three Loyalty Models

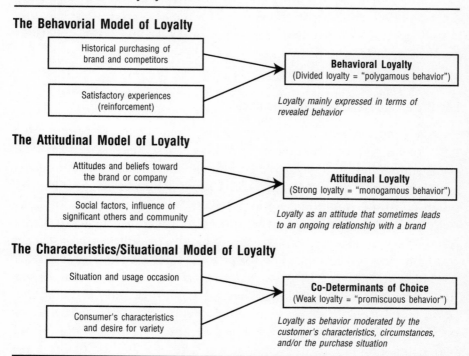

Source: Adapted from Mark D. Uncles, Grahame R. Dowling, and Kathy Hammond, "Customer Loyalty and Customer Loyalty Programs," *Journal of Consumer Marketing* 20, no. 4 (2003), 294–316. Used with permission, Emerald Publishing Group Limited.

Loyalty as Purchases

Much of what we know about loyalty has come from the study of purchasing behavior. The consumer panels maintained by the *Chicago Tribune* and reported on by George Brown, a *Tribune* marketing researcher, were some of the earlier and more publicized attempts to track loyalty.[5] Using self-reported purchases (recorded in diaries), Brown and his colleagues created the notion of sequences of purchases (brand runs). They identified three basic formations: AAAAAA, loyalty; ABABAB, divided loyalty; and unstable loyalty, AAABBB. Brown's work was the legacy to today's scanner panels hosted by ACNielsen and Information Resources, Inc. (IRI). Using the past-purchase information, probabilities are generated for each brand for the next purchase occasion.

Behavioral models are purely historical and deterministic. They shed no understanding on the reasons for the observed behavior; they simply produce probabilities for future purchases based on what has been recorded in the past.

Loyalty as the Result of Circumstances

This is a moderation view. It rationalizes that while consumers may have feelings about brands or suppliers, these may not always be compelling enough to override certain situational factors (often characterized in the other approaches as *contingency variables*). Hence, when consumer preferences are not well defined, they may be *constructed* based on the influence of these contingency factors.[6] Three types of contingency variables are specified: *consumer circumstances* (budget, time constraints, need for novelty, tolerance for risk, need for social approval, etc.); *consumer characteristics* (such as habit, desire for variety, tolerance of risk, and need to conform); and *purchase situation effects* (including product availability, promotions/deals, the use occasion). Resulting choices are therefore affected by the trade-off between consumer goals, the effort it will take to make the choice, and influences from the purchase situation.[7] In the words of Uncles, Dowling, and Hammond, "The difference between this contingency per-

Source: Cartoonybin.com. Reproduced with permission.

spective and the attitude perspective is that the contingency factors are elevated from the status of loyalty inhibitors in Model 1 to loyalty co-determinants in Model 3."[8]

WHEN DOES LOYALTY OCCUR?

Consumers make many purchase decisions each day. Not all of these decisions are of equal importance, and not all receive the same degree of consideration. Three different levels of decision making have generally been accepted based on a model first proposed by John Howard.[9] These decision-making levels have to do with how much active consideration (sometimes called *information processing*) the consumer invests in a particular purchase choice. Other factors influencing the amount of consideration a consumer invests in any particular purchase decision include:

- The *importance* and *nature* of the product or service being considered.
- The *frequency* with which the purchase has previously been made.
- The *complexity* of the product or service and its purchase.

The types of resulting decisions range from *extensive* consideration, through *limited*, to *knee-jerk reactions.*

Another way purchases can be compared is by how personally captivating (or involving) the item being purchased is. Some product purchases are inherently quite involving (like the purchase of a new convertible automobile); others are inconsequential (a purchase of new socks or hosiery). In the Introduction, we highlighted one of the factors generally agreed to influence the degree of personal involvement in the purchase consideration, that being risk (and its many faces).

These two criteria, *amount of consideration* and *degree of involvement*, can be used to construct a two-way grid, shown in Figure 7.2 that succinctly includes most consumer purchases. The resulting quadrants of the grid delineate the four approaches to purchases that consumers employ. The lower right, characterized by knee-jerk (reflexive) purchasing, pertains to low-involvement products and services. Here previous purchases have been rewarded, and the likelihood of them being continued increases. The type of learning that has occurred is most similar to classical learning theory and is analogous to a monkey repeatedly hitting a lever because previous hits have produced a piece of banana (the infamous "chimp-o-mat"). If there is any conscious evaluation of the chosen alternative, it occurs after purchase.

In direct contrast, the upper left includes high-involvement products and services, perhaps being purchased for the first time. Here the consumer engages in the most studied problem solving—collecting information, evaluating it, and ultimately making the purchase thought

FIGURE 7.2   Types of Decisions

	High Involvement	Low Involvement

Active Decision Making	**Intensive Decision Making**
	Sequence:
	  Beliefs formed
	  Evaluation
	  Purchase
	Cognitive Learning
		Limited Decision Making
		Sequence:
		  Beliefs formed
		  Purchase
		  Evaluation
		Passive Learning

Acts Historically	**Brand Loyalty**
	Sequence:
	  (Beliefs formed)
	  (Evaluation)
	  Purchase
	Instrumental Conditioning
		Rote Purchasing
		Sequence:
		  Beliefs formed
		  Purchase
		  Evaluation
		Classical Conditioning

Source: Henry Assael, *Consumer Behavior: A Strategic Approach*, Boston: Houghton Mifflin, 2003, Figure 41, page 100. Used with permission.

to maximize his or her benefits. The theory of learning most representative of this decision making process is cognitive learning theory. Once the risks of high-involvement products and services have been conquered (with a successful purchase), consumers generally migrate to the lower left, the quadrant representing loyalty. The learning theory explaining such loyal behavior is said to be instrumental learning theory—satisfaction with the brand purchased has positively reinforced the association with the brand, resulting in a high likelihood of the brand being purchased repetitively in the future.

Many people are surprised to find loyalty associated with high-involvement purchases. A common misperception may be that repetitive behavior, quasi loyalty, is relegated to those purchases that are neither very involving nor very important; but they are so uninvolving that the same brand is routinely purchased without much thought or commitment. We refer to this behavior expressed towards low-involvement products and services as rote purchasing. Loyalty, on the other hand, is a way to minimize risk in highly involving purchase situations.

Because of the critical role of involvement, for decades marketers have tried to manipulate consumers' involvement either with their particular brand or with the product category to which their brand belongs.

MANIPULATING CONSUMER INVOLVEMENT

For functionally superior products or products new to a category, it is beneficial to stimulate as much conscious decision making as possible. One way marketers have attempted to do this is by manipulating the involvement consumers allocate to a category or a purchase. This can be accomplished by:

- Increasing the purchase's importance for the consumer.
- Adding emotional significance to the purchase.
- Associating the purchase with an ongoing interest.
- Attaching significant risks to the purchase.
- Associating the purchase with a relevant reference group.

Any success in increasing involvement would be constructive in fostering loyalty.

The Australian Broadcasting Corporation's (ABC-TV) television series *Fat Cow Motel* is a remarkable example of creatively building audience involvement.[10] Unlike more traditional TV dramas, each of the 13 episodes of *Fat Cow Motel* required the audience to solve a mystery, with the correct solution revealed in the following week's episode. For traditional television viewers, enough clues were provided within each episode to solve that week's mystery. For more modern viewers familiar with multiple media platforms additional clues were made available via an interactive web site, e-mail, short messaging service (SMS) and interactive television (iTV).

Through the invited interactivity, FatCowMotel.com became the most visited television-related web site in the seven-year history of *ABC-TV Online*, receiving a record 1.2 million visits in the program's second week on ABC-TV (the week ending Sunday, July 20, 2003).[11] Since setting this record, the site has continued to receive over half a million visits a week, making it the most visited TV web site ever on ABC-TV Online.

THE ROLE OF BRANDS AND COMPANIES

While loyalty rests in the consumer, it requires a clearly defined target. Brands and corporate entities are what make loyalty possible. In marketing's brief history, disproportionate attention has been directed to the brand, sometimes in the form of industrywide surveys. The *Business Week* Global Brand Valuation is one such study.[12] According to this source, of the 2004 most highly valued brands, Coca-Cola was ranked first with an estimated total *brand name value* of $64 billion; Microsoft was runner up at $61 billion, while IBM received third place

Source: Cartoonybin.com. Reproduced with permission.

with a whopping $53 billion. Brian's favorite, Heinz, came out 42nd with a brand name value of $7 billion.

Mathematically, brand name value is easily defined. Using a formula perspective, calculations determining the brand name value (employing criteria such as the net present value of projected future sales revenue streams) are relatively easy to understand. But the reality is that customer loyalty for a brand is what lies beneath the continued revenue streams and, therefore, determines brand name value. Without such continued preference (in the form of a loyal customer base), it is not possible for brands to create and sustain such value.

ROLE OF THE SERVICE EXPERIENCE IN LOYALTY

While the brand plays a very important role in forming loyalty, other elements may be important as well. If a product incorporates a service experience or is a service itself, then satisfaction with components of the service experience may also influence customers' loyalty. In conceptualizing loyalty for such products, the service experience should be included.

Consider our homemaker Elaine's selection of her favorite supermarket at which to shop. Unless she hires a babysitter, her two children probably accompany her to the grocery store. Hence, how child-friendly a supermarket is would probably have a big influence on her store loyalty. Providing a way to integrate her children into the shopping experience by providing mini shopping carts or a child seat attachable to the cart or even providing balloons for the kids could all be important in making the chore less stressful for Elaine and more enjoyable for her children. This, in turn, could translate into increased satisfaction and become instrumental in making her loyal to a particular store.

JOINT EFFECTS OF BRAND AND SERVICE EXPERIENCE ON LOYALTY: 2 + 2 = 5

Traditionally in research, the concepts of "brand" and "customer" have been considered separately. In industry practice, they have been separated even further, as the responsibilities of different departments within organizations. Consequently, the field of marketing has bifurcated into two divisions: product management and consumer behavior. Only recently have managers begun to consider how these two areas might interrelate.

The authors of this book have conducted studies to test the independence of brand measures from customer satisfaction. These studies have overturned conventional thinking by showing a remarkable *interdependence* heretofore not acknowledged. While both measures (brand preference and customer satisfaction) contribute individually to loyalty, when satisfaction increases are considered in conjunction with brand preference, the effect on loyalty is exponential.

To gain insight into the relationship between brand-centric and customer-centric measures, the authors used data from two disparate industries: institutional banking and fleet truck manufacturing.[13] For the institutional banking industry, the effect of the combined measures on loyalty doubles that of either measure alone. Figure 7.3 shows results from the fleet trucking industry. The effect of customer satisfaction by itself on repurchase was 8 percent; the effect of brand preference by itself was 11 percent. But these two factors combined resulted in a 21 percent impact on repurchase. Two plus two may sometimes exceed four! This example dramatically illustrates the interdependency of customer metrics and brand metrics.

THE CONSIDERATION SET

While managers would like to think that consumers conscientiously evaluate the benefits of competing brands in every purchase situation before making their choice, our previous discussion of the three levels of decision making (intensive, moderate, and knee-jerk) suggests otherwise. Compounding efficient decision making is the staggering number of alternatives consumers may select from in any given product category. To simplify what might otherwise become a daunting task, consumers have adopted a process that eases the burden of decision making. One such process widely recognized by

FIGURE 7.3 Brand-Satisfaction Interaction

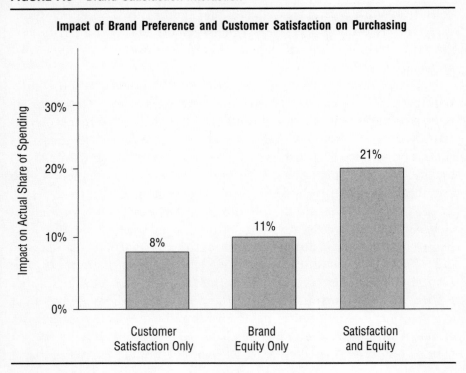

Impact of Brand Preference and Customer Satisfaction on Purchasing

theorists is the "consideration set" process, which is illustrated in Figure 7.4.

The consideration set (or evoked set) is the result of a funneling process that immensely simplifies customers' purchasing activities. When considering any product or service category, there are a great number of alternatives available to consumers. Typically, consumers are aware of only a subset of the alternatives that exist in the marketplace. In Figure 7.4, the second column from the left lists those brands from all available (first column) of which the consumer is aware—the *awareness set*. One or more of these may be rejected from further consideration because of something the consumer has heard or because of a previous poor experience with the brand. These brands are identified in the third column, the *inept set* (rejected alternatives). Of the remaining brands, some will be so un-

FIGURE 7.4 Consideration Set Process

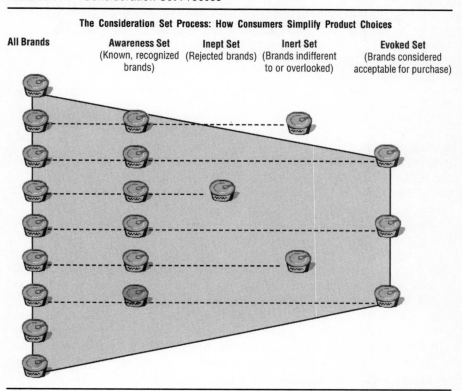

The Consideration Set Process: How Consumers Simplify Product Choices

| All Brands | Awareness Set (Known, recognized brands) | Inept Set (Rejected brands) | Inert Set (Brands indifferent to or overlooked) | Evoked Set (Brands considered acceptable for purchase) |

familiar that they are momentarily set aside, while other brands may evoke indifference. Both of these situations are covered by the fourth column, the *indifference set*. This funneling process leaves the consumer with the fifth column, in this case a manageable three brands that are each acceptable for purchase. These final three brands represent the *evoked set* (the subset of brands that will be considered for purchase on any given purchase occasion).

Securing consumers' attention and market share becomes quite daunting, given that consumers typically include only two to three alternatives in their evoked sets for most product and service categories. Figure 7.5 summarizes the results of published studies that have assessed the mean number of alternatives typically included in

FIGURE 7.5 Average Size of Consideration Sets

The Average Consideration Set Size for Various Products and Services

Category	Average Consideration Set Size	Category	Average Consideration Set Size
Antacid[a]	3.0	Deodorant[g]	3.0
Autos (USA)[b]	8.1	Dishwashing liquid[f]	5.6
Autos (Norway)[c]	2.0	Gasoline[h]	3.0
Auto maintenance[d]	1.7	Margarine[e]	4.3
Barber/Beauty[d]	1.6	Pain relievers[a]	3.0
Beer (USA)[e]	2.6	Shampoo[a]	4.0
Beer (Canada)[a]	7.0	Soft drinks[h]	5.0
Coffee[f]	4.2	Table napkins[f]	5.0

[a]Glen L. Urban, "Perceptor: A Model for Product Positioning," *Management Science* 6, no. 2 (1975), 182–201.
[b]John R. Hauser, Glen L. Urban, and John H. Roberts, "Forecasting Sales of a New Consumer Durable," in *Advances and Practices of Marketing Science*, ed. Fred S. Zufryden (Providence, RI: The Institute of Management Science 1983), 115–128.
[c]Kjell Grønhaug, "Some Factors in Influencing the Size of the Buyer's Evoked Set," *European Journal of Marketing* 7 (Winter 1973/1974), 232–241.
[d]L.W. Turley and Ronald R. LeBlanc, "An Exploratory Investigation of Consumer Decision Making in the Service Sector," *Journal of Services Marketing* 7, no. 4 (1993), 11–18.
[e]Berend Wierenga, *An Investigation of Brand Choice and Processes* (Rotterdam, The Netherlands: Rotterdam University Press, 1974).
[f]Lance P. Jarvis and James B. Wilcox, "Evoked Set Size—Some Theoretical Foundations and Empirical Evidence," in *Increasing Marketing Productivity and Conceptual and Methodological Foundations of Marketing* (AMA Combined Proceedings), vol. 35, ed. Thomas V. Greer (Chicago: American Marketing Association 1973), 236–240.
[g]Alvin J. Silk and Glen L. Urban, "Pre-Test Market Evaluation of New Packaged Goods: A Model and Measurement Methodology," *Journal of Marketing Research* 15 (May 1978), 171–191.
[h]Juanita J. Brown and Albert R. Wildt, "Consideration Set Measurement," *Journal of the Academy of Marketing Science* 20, no. 3 (Summer 1992), 235–243.

the evoked (consideration) sets for many categories within different countries.

The challenge all organizations face is to have their brand(s) become one of the fortunate, considered alternatives in the evoked set. This is an obvious prerequisite for a legitimate shot at being selected for purchase, regardless of the frequency of the purchase. Without a doubt, many factors influence a brand's inclusion in a customer's evoked set. Prior positive experiences, referrals from friends and family, general promotion activities, and even point-of-purchase stimuli can all be potential factors for inclusion. For a particular product to have a chance at being included in the consideration set for a particular product category, however, the product has to be perceived as belonging to *that category*.

Getting into Customers' Consideration Sets

Consumers' processes of categorizing products and brands make *positioning* of a product crucial to its ultimate inclusion in the consideration set. PepsiCo is one of many companies that found this out the hard way. In the early 1980s, Pepsico introduced a new beverage called Pepsi A.M. This new product concept was the result of an increasing number of late-teen and 20-year-olds drinking caffeinated colas for breakfast rather than coffee. The name, however, caused consumers to interpret it as only a morning beverage, and so they did not consider it when choosing a beverage to be consumed at other times of the day. Needless to say, Pepsi A.M.'s product life cycle was short lived.[14]

General Mills committed a similar error with its introduction of cranberry-orange and mandarin-orange Jell-O Gelatin Flavors for Salad. Because of the inclusion of the words "for salad" in the brand name, consumers apparently relegated the product for use exclusively in salads. Consequently, they excluded this brand extension from their consideration sets for potential dessert options, even though this product was no different from other regular Jell-O products, other than being new flavors.

Gaining Preference

After successfully being included in a consumer's consideration set, the next step is to increase the preference of your brand over the others in the set. When consumers engage in extensive or moderate decision making, they attempt, albeit informally, to maximize their expected outcomes by selecting the brand or alternative from their evoked set that promises the greatest potential benefits. They do this through a kind of hedonistic calculus in which they mentally compare brands by their belief in the brands' ability to deliver various attributes, weighted by how valuable these attributes are. A perspective called customer value management (CVA) has developed around this process. The problem is that, as CVA is currently practiced, it allows the absence of one variable to be compensated by another variable. This is called a *compensatory* calculation. In reality, consumers seek attributes in a hierarchical order, negating much of the predictive value of CVA analyses.

Because their preferences are not always well defined, consumers are said to exercise "bounded rationality" and hence employ limited information processing capacities.[15] For most of the choices they make, preferences are usually not well formed but are *constructed* using a variety of strategies contingent upon the task required, the social context, and their own idiosyncrasies.[16]

Products are not evaluated in isolation. Alternative products are important influences when consumers determine the relative attractiveness of any product. Professor Itamar Simonson from Stanford University illustrates this comparative phenomenon by citing a simple but interesting example.[17] Individuals, in groups, were asked to make a choice between receiving an expensive Cross pen or $6 in cash. Other groups were asked to make a similar choice, except this time, the consideration set was expanded to include a less attractive pen along with the Cross pen and the cash. The proportion of individuals choosing cash over the pen was not the main focus of the study. What was interesting was the *change* in the proportion of subjects choosing the pen to those choosing cash. There was a significant increase in the proportion of people choosing the Cross pen over cash in the second group. Although the less attractive pen was not destined to be chosen, its mere presence in the consideration set affected the attractiveness of the other alternative, making the Cross pen more desirable and the cash less appealing.

What does this mean for marketing managers? It demonstrates the importance of understanding (1) the other alternatives consumers consider, (2) how important various attributes of the product category are to the consumer and how the various alternative products score on those alternatives, and (3) how the attractiveness of a brand can be changed as inferior or superior alternatives enter the category.

Another approach to fostering stronger preference for a brand is to create additional differentiation. Traditional loyalty and frequency programs can offer some differentiation. An example of such programs is the Air Miles loyalty program operating in the UK, Canada, the Netherlands, and the United Arab Emirates. In 1988, when the program launched in the UK, more than 130 companies signed on as sponsors. After three years of operation, Air Miles had more than four million members and claimed $40 million in accumulated revenue. The program can claim participation by world-recognized marketers including Shell, Hertz, and NatWest Bank. Some of these large organizations actually opted for participation in the Air Miles program over running their own program.

Source: Cartoonybin.com. Reproduced with permission.

The business model for the program seems logical. British Airways, the program's principal redemptions airline (and 51 percent owner), makes surplus seat inventory available to Air Miles at a discounted fee. Sponsoring companies reward miles differently according to the type and value of the purchases that customer-members make. For example, a member might buy a Toshiba television set for €400 and earn an air mile for each euro, and then, by using a NatWest Visa or Access credit card, earn one mile for each €20 charged. Since each reward mile equals one mile of air travel, members know approximately their range of travel at any given moment. To redeem miles they simply contact Air Miles. A fringe benefit is the stimulation of auxiliary travel needs among members, and the value of the transaction-detailed database being added to on a daily basis.

LIMITATIONS OF BEHAVIORAL LOYALTY MEASURES: CONTINUED PURCHASE DOES NOT NECESSARILY EQUAL LOYALTY

Does continued preference always translate into loyalty? No. There are at least three conditions under which continued preference does not necessarily denote loyalty.

1. *High costs of change:* In some cases there is a direct cost associated with customers discontinuing a relationship. For example, customers may have made investments in equipment that is not compatible with competing systems or is costly to replace (such as gas versus electric heating). Even when the actual economic costs are low, there is usually a time cost for customers associated with terminating a relationship. Whether it be the time required to physically close a relationship and start another (for example, changing insurance companies) or simply the time required to learn about competitive alternatives, time costs virtually always provide a retention advantage to the incumbent firm.

2. *High Risks of Change:* Customers may perceive a heightened risk associated with leaving. For example, a bank customer may worry whether a new bank will be as careful in processing her checks as the current one. Equally important are worries about whether the new product will perform as well as the current one or will conform to its specifications.

3. *Self-Protection and Change:* In a number of industries, it is not in customers' best interests to maintain monogamous relationships. For example, manufacturers, in their role as customers, have long known it is dangerous to single-source their most critical components. For this reason businesses have tended to maintain polygamous business relationships to lower their risk, keep costs in check, and, in so doing, gain information regarding product and process innovation. Consumers are similarly sophisticated, inherently recognizing that it is in their economic interests to maintain multiple relationships in a variety of different categories. For example, knowing that alternatives exist, we may say, "I will buy this elsewhere, because I can get it cheaper, faster, better-serviced there."

Additionally, some consumers enjoy the psychological benefit of variety seeking, derived from experiencing substitute vendors by maintaining polygamous business relationships.

USING "RELATIONSHIP QUALITY" AS AN ALTERNATE APPROACH TO BECOMING THE PREFERRED BRAND

Customer loyalty can be thought of as evolving from *casual acquaintanceships* with brands or service providers to *committed partnerships* with these entities. Consumer attachments to brands can be classified into some of the following categories:

- *Personal identity*. This relationship type portrays the degree to which the brand is instrumental in expressing a significant part of who you are.
- *Interdependence*. This relationship type portrays the degree to which the brand is entrenched in the daily life of the consumer. For example, the success of the "Got Milk" campaign is partly based on the discovery that consumers maintain an interdependence type of relationship with their milk.

- *Nostalgia.* This relationship is based on an attachment to the brand caused by connections to the past, such as childhood memories.

- *Commitment.* This type of relationship includes a dedication to the continuity of the relationship despite possible unfavorable circumstances.

- *Love/passion.* The brand that inspires such feelings is frequently believed to be irreplaceable and elicits adoration of the brand (think Harley-Davidson motorcycle owners).

- *Intimacy.* This relationship is portrayed by a deep sense of familiarity with the brand and the impression that it is a partner.[18]

ARE CONSUMER CHARACTERISTICS INFLUENTIAL IN INCREASING PROPENSITY TO BRAND LOYALTY?

Several researchers have attempted to define the characteristics of a brand-loyal consumer. Their studies have shown there is not a generalized loyal-customer type. Brand loyalty tends to be specific to product classes, not consumers. However, some demographic generalizations have been offered to point to consumers who may be more loyalty prone:

- Consumers prone to brand loyalty tend to be more self-confident in their choices of products and brands.

- Brand-loyal consumers are likely to perceive a higher degree of risk associated with the product or product class.

- Minority group consumers have been shown to be more brand loyal. (This may also be related to financial risk.)

Though these consumer characteristics offer some guidance, in general, product characteristics will outweigh consumer characteristics in defining loyalty.

CLASSIFYING CONSUMERS BASED
ON THEIR LEVEL OF BRAND LOYALTY

If one were to examine a large population of consumer purchases in a typical product category, researchers Uncles, Dowling, and Hammond contend that the purchasing consumers could likely be segmented into three groups according to the loyalty model that defined their buying behavior. They postulate three consumer types:

- Consumer brand acceptance (CBA).
- Consumer brand commitment (CBC).
- Consumer brand buying (CBB).[19]

Consumer brand acceptance (CBA), they argue, would account for the majority of consumers in most purchase situations. They propose that the loyalty definition underlying these consumers' brand choice is essentially *loyalty as a behavior*. These consumers see little reason for forming monogamous relationships with single brands, largely because the leading brands in most categories rarely exhibit substantial differences. The proliferation of products has ameliorated brand distinctiveness. Even advertising and loyalty offers for these brands will have become homogenized. Need triggers the category purchase; brand selection will be swayed by both familiarity and availability. Consideration sets are the ticket to play for these consumers.

The two remaining loyalty styles are seen by Uncles, Dowling, and Hammond as exceptions, not as the rule—which is contrary to the prevailing conception. Consumer brand commitment (CBC) is a dedication to a brand. Here *loyalty as a feeling* is the associated definition. Consumers within this segment value the psychological and social benefits of a brand more than its functionality. This type of brand selection behavior is easiest to observe (and perhaps understand as well) with high-identity, luxury goods. Unlike the commoditized brands that drive the CBA consumer, CBC consumers are attracted to brands with considerable distinctiveness, caché, and edge. Examples include the Apple Macintosh computer, the Sony Walkman, the Blackberry PDA, Williams-Sonoma stores, and Mercedes-Benz automobiles.

Source: Cartoonybin.com. Reproduced with permission.

These consumers will gladly form monogamous relationships with brands and will invest of themselves to do so.

The final segment, consumer brand buying (CBB), is typical of our third definition of loyalty: loyalty determined by circumstances. Consumers in this segment exhibit very low levels of pure brand loyalty; they tend to be more loyal to circumstances than to brands. That means their selection at any purchase occasion will be more a function of price, promotions, and availability than of any specific brand's appeal.

A NEED TO EXAMINE THE EFFICACY OF CURRENT POPULAR TOOLS IN THE MEASUREMENT OF LOYALTY: RFM

There is clearly a general lack of understanding of what loyalty means. Does this lack of understanding apply to the *measurement* of loyalty as well? To gain deeper insight, let us turn to one of the most popular techniques used to identify loyal customers. The "recency, frequency, and monetary value" (RFM) approach has, in fact, been one of the most widely used methods to identify loyal customers for the past 30 years—particularly by direct marketers, and especially by nonprofits.[20] Based on the assumption that past purchase behavior can be used to predict future behavior, this approach uses three variables to differentiate loyal and nonloyal customers: Recency (R) describes how recently the customer made a purchase; frequency (F) describes how frequently the customer buys; and monetary value (M) identifies how much the customer has spent. The assumption is that the most recent, most frequent, and largest-spending customers are the best customers since it is assumed they will act similarly in the future as well.

The stages in a typical RFM analysis include sorting the database in descending order by the three variables. The database is then divided into quintiles or deciles (depending on how large the database is) for each variable, and each customer is assigned an RFM code that describes where they fall in the database relative to other customers. That the RFM technique is so popular is not happenstance. Most companies keep track of this data, making it easily accessible, and no specialized software is needed to conduct the analysis since it is based essentially on a simple indication of quintiles and a subsequent ranking of the three-digit code indicating the quintile of each component. In the case of data broken into quintiles, 125 segments of the customer base are produced (5^3). Hence an RFM code of 111 would describe the best customers, as they would be the group with the highest quintiles of purchase recency, purchase frequency, and money spent.

There are, however, some serious drawbacks to this approach that can be misleading. First, RFM is primarily a segmentation scheme, assigning customers to a group rather than calculating an individual score for each customer. Second, there is an inherent bias toward focusing solely on the best customers.[21] In this vein, RFM has been considered exploitative because it mandates focusing on those who already have spent the most. It fails to consider potential or developmental growth.

The biggest problem with RFM is its assumption that how recently, how frequently, and how much a customer spends are the *only* three variables that determine the value of a customer. An accurate approach to loyalty should take all factors that determine loyalty into consideration when conducting its measurement.

Given that numerous other factors noticeably influence the reasons that consumers prefer products, the fact that the RFM technique cannot possibly do a good job of capturing loyalty should not come as a surprise. The lack of correspondence between the causes of customer loyalty and the attributes used to measure it will undoubtedly do a poor job of predicting customer loyalty.

A NEED TO REVISE TRADITIONAL LOYALTY MEASURES

Obviously there is a need to change the way loyalty has traditionally been measured. The main argument is not that behavioral measures are incorrect, but rather that they are incomplete. Understanding consumer behavior, how individuals form their preferences, and the factors that influence the strength of these preferences should guide managers into an awareness of the crucial steps that need to be taken with regard to loyalty measurement.

But there is more to measuring loyalty than solely taking a behavioral approach. It is imperative that more attitudinal and emotion-laden components be melded into the definition of loyalty. Where these factors are not considered, it may not be possible to measure loyalty accurately. This realization has two important implications for managers:

1. The first question managers must answer is, "What data should be collected from the customer to make a more accurate assessment of his or her loyalty status, and where, how, and when should this data be collected?"

2. If loyalty is based mostly on meanings that are ascribed to a product, loyalty programs should focus on instilling those meanings rather on than encouraging customers to come again by offering them repeat benefits. This shift in emphasis will directly influence decisions about investment to foster customer loyalty.

SETTING THE RECORD STRAIGHT:
THE FOUNDATIONS OF CUSTOMER LOYALTY

Marketers are frequently criticized by the public with accusations like "Marketers try to manipulate consumers by making consumers think brands are important." Is Elaine really being manipulated into buying Heinz ketchup? Why *should* consumers care about brands? What is the benefit and function of brands? To answer this question, it may be helpful to think what it would be like if we did not have brands.

Even if the world wasn't as stark as that of *Repo Man*, Elaine would still walk into the grocery store and find herself in front of the ketchup aisle, reaching out for one of the many ketchup products displayed on the shelf. She would likely examine the price, packaging, and content label of the product to help her make a decision, and would repeat this for the various ketchup products on the shelf. Assuming that she handled at least four different ketchup products, it would take her considerable time to arrive at a final choice. Not knowing what to expect from this product, she may experience some mild discomfort with her choice. Could Elaine trust this company to adhere to the highest quality standards? Would this ketchup taste good? Would her nine-year-old son Brian like it?

The fact is that brands actually add value to our lives, in at least five ways:

1. *Brands are cues*. They embody certain associations with the product. Our lives require capitalizing on cues because we almost never have complete information to make a fully informed judgment. Just as the famous Sherlock Holmes looked to people's clothes, posture, and style of speech to infer their profession and background, in the absence of sufficient and complete information, we, too, look to the observable, or known, to infer a judgment about the unknown. Our associations with a brand enable us to make a judgment about it and form an idea of what to expect. Brands are even more important in the online environment, where it is difficult and sometimes impossible to gather other information about the product prior to making a choice—information that we would normally obtain by handling the product, smelling it, or feeling it. In this context, brands can be an important cue to infer judgments.

2. *Brands save us time.* We may also not *want* to spend the time and effort to gather the information necessary to make a choice based on complete information. Elaine saves a lot of time, knowing what Heinz stands for. She does not have to examine all the ketchup products before arriving at a choice. Being a housewife and mother of two is already quite demanding. Anything that makes her life easier is probably appreciated.

3. *Brands make us comfortable.* Elaine is comfortable with her Heinz choice. Why? Because she knows that she will get the same taste with each bottle she buys. This consistency of taste gives her peace of mind, because it eliminates the risk of ruining the family's favorite dish. Elaine also feels comfortable knowing that Heinz adheres to the highest quality standards in terms of food safety. She trusts the brand and knows that no one will fall ill because of Heinz ketchup.

4. *Brands are a vehicle to express ourselves.* We may prefer to express our standing for or even against a certain product or issue via our preferred brands. Elaine may prefer Heinz because it was the ketchup found on the table in her parents' kitchen when she was growing up. Her preference hence could be a vehicle to express her inherent connection to tradition and her childhood.

5. *Brands could help us make better choices.* Imagine Elaine pressed for time on her weekly shopping trip. Her familiarity with the Heinz brand helps her make a better choice because she has avoided the risk of making a bad choice.

All of that might sound like corny, pro-corporate hype. Without question, we as consumers are bombarded with corporate messages attempting to establish new brands in our lives and influence our loyalty. Still, it is far better than the world of *Repo Man*. In the end, companies' efforts to establish brands as reliable answers to our needs are more of a blessing than we typically realize.

As we noted earlier, there are at least two factions within marketing, the brand perspective and the customer perspective. These approaches have largely been managed independently from each other.

Our investigations show how interdependent the brand and customer approaches are. In hindsight, this is exactly how one might suspect that things would work.

Loyalty Truth 7: Customer loyalty and brand imagery are far from independent; you must manage them hand-in-hand.

While brand and customer form a dyadic relationship, recent work in consumer behavior is extending the paradigm to include even more factors. It is critical for the loyalty professional to become familiar with these additional factors.

The Right Way to Manage for Customer Loyalty

Appreciation is expressed to V. Kumar, who contributed to the writing of this chapter. Roland T. Rust is acknowledged for his writings that have immensely benefited the evolution of loyalty theory and application.[1]

Absorb what is useful. Reject what is useless. Add what is specifically your own.[2]

> —Lee Jun Fan (aka Bruce Lee, martial arts
> master and movie star)

Playwright and author Oscar Wilde observed, "The truth is rarely pure and never simple."[3] Having disposed of some of the most pervasive myths about customer loyalty in the preceding chapters, we find Wilde's observation particularly appropriate. Learning of Al "Chainsaw" Dunlap's, Michael O'Leary's, and Jerry Jurgensen's successes despite applying the antitheses of customer loyalty strategies, it would be easy to conclude that the best approach to running a business is to abandon any pursuit of customer loyalty.

Without question, it is possible to make money, at least in the short term, by focusing on cost reduction and ignoring customer loyalty, as Dunlap's, O'Leary's, and Jurgensen's stories demonstrate. And, unfortunately, there is no guarantee that focusing on strengthening customer loyalty will guarantee success. Even if an executive is sold on customer loyalty as a long-term strategy, she may still lose lots of money if her developed strategy is based on a naïve reliance on one or more of the loyalty myths. But neither of these outcomes should be construed as suggesting that customer loyalty as a business strategy is wrong. In fact, when it is based on sound foundations, we believe that building customer loyalty can be a very profitable business strategy.

It is human nature to totally dismiss a philosophy when we learn that some or much of what we have been told about it is wrong. While understandable, such a posture is an obvious mistake. The science associated with customer loyalty as a business strategy is relatively new and rapidly evolving. Our current knowledge has advanced to the point of finding flaws in the conventional positions—the myths. More important, we can use the evolving science to demonstrate and prove our "loyalty truths" that we've associated with profitable customer loyalty strategies.

To dismiss loyalty as a viable strategy because of the fallacious myths associated with it is to throw the baby out with the bathwater. "When people thought the Earth was flat, they were wrong. When people thought the Earth was spherical, they were [still] wrong," observed author and professor Isaac Asimov. "But if you think that thinking the Earth is spherical is just as wrong as thinking the Earth is flat, then your view is wronger than both of them put together."[4]

Here is a review of the truths of customer loyalty that summarized each of Chapters 1 through 7. While the truths of customer loyalty are not nearly as simple as the myths, they offer basic insights into the true workings of customer loyalty.

The Seven Truths of Customer Loyalty

1. Don't manage for customer retention before you manage for customer selection.

2. Customer loyalty takes more time to grow than most management teams have to give; planning and patience are required.

3. Focus on customers' share-of-wallet. Don't disregard those customers with current low shares; consumer polygamy is the rule these days. But don't accept your current share. Learn how to improve your share of your customers' loyalty.

4. Loyalty requires mutually beneficial interactions; most loyalty programs are tilted in the company's favor.

5. The chain of events from loyalty to profits is twisted and complex. Learn the specific response patterns of your customers and your industry.

6. Satisfied and loyal employees can make a difference, but customer satisfaction and loyalty can and often does happen in the absence of employee satisfaction and loyalty.

7. Customer loyalty and brand imagery are far from independent; you must manage them hand-in-hand.

For the next several pages, we'll elaborate on each of these mandates, helping the reader to better institute a profitable customer loyalty strategy at his company.

LOYALTY TRUTH 1: DON'T MANAGE FOR CUSTOMER RETENTION BEFORE YOU MANAGE FOR CUSTOMER SELECTION

There are many socially redeeming benefits from adopting a customer loyalty strategy. It requires a firm to treat all its constituencies with dignity, and to establish a corporate climate that supports, expects, and rewards customer service and unrelentingly seeks new ways to enhance peoples' lives. Nevertheless, while all of this is good, the ultimate goal of any corporate initiative, including those designed to enhance customer loyalty, must be to generate profits.

The reality is that not all customers want or are willing to pay whatever added costs may be required to provide them a pleasant relationship. In addition, some customers simply do not generate an adequate rate of return to justify their participation in an enhanced relationship. Moreover, many customers are just plain unprofitable—making an expense on their behalf unthinkable. When you look at a customer base in this way, it is terrifying to consider how most loyalty initiatives have simple-mindedly been extended to *entire* customer bases! We need to remind ourselves that each of our customers either adds to or subtracts from the financial health of our enterprise. Therefore, it is essential that we gauge each customer's profitability before implementing *any* loyalty effort.[5]

Attempts to identify best customers are certainly not new, as we have mentioned earlier; the direct marketing industry is completely oriented to best customers. The problem faced by today's marketers is that virtually none of the conventional methods does a good job. Many measures like RFM (recency, frequency, monetary value, discussed in Chapter 7) rely on past or current profitability. But even when a method is right, the data may be wrong. In many other cases, customer profitability (current or historical) is paradoxically incalculable, and managers have to rely on proxies such as revenue. Unfortunately, as we pointed out in Myth 46, customer revenue is not a good predictor of customer profitability.

What is needed is a forward-looking measure of customer profitability: the expected profits to be derived from customer relationships, starting at the current time period and projected out to a managerially relevant point in the future. We have a good starting point. A reasonably young concept in marketing is customer lifetime value (CLV), generally implemented as the stream of purchases a customer is likely to make in her "lifetime" of transactions with a firm.[6] We will make three important modifications, which have been suggested by Venkatesan and Kumar:[7]

1. Rather than adopt the average lifetime value of an enterprise's customers, we'll calculate lifetime values at the disaggregate level of the individual customer.

2. We will forgo the practice of adopting the average lifetime (the complete lifespan of the customer with the company, the number of purchase cycles or time over which the customer is expected to continue his relationship with the organization). Instead, we'll adopt a shorter, more pragmatic time frame, typically three years. This will need to be extended by

durables manufacturers for whom repurchase cycles are notably longer.

3. Our CLV will be entirely predictive, reaching out into the future. To distinguish this CLV from the more common, historical CLV, we'll label our CLV as "CLV_f."

CLV_f defined: The net present value of a customer's cumulative profits over his/her lifetime with the company. (The time horizon is limited to three years for managerial relevance.)

The key components of calculating CLV_f are customer acquisition and retention costs. The other main elements are the gross contribution each customer provides and the marketing costs that are incurred for every customer in each time period.

There are a number of reasons that CLV_f is essential to the optimal implementation of a customer loyalty initiative:

▪ It is a forward-looking metric, unlike other traditional measures (which include past contribution to profit).

▪ It helps marketers adopt the right marketing activities today to increase future profitability.

▪ It is the only metric that incorporates all the elements of revenue, expense, and customer behavior that drive profitability.

▪ It enforces the focus on the customer (instead of products) as the driver of profitability.

CLV_f is a metric superior to traditional, commonly used measures to identify the most attractive customers, such as RFM and contribution to profits.[8] None of these measures is forward looking and none focuses on *expected profitability* of the customer (with the exception of contribution to profits, which focuses on *past profits*). These measures are contrasted in Figure 8.1.

By knowing a customer's expected CLV_f, it becomes possible to set an upper threshold for investing in loyalty without running the risk of overspending. For example, suppose the CLV_f for a customer with a high likelihood of defecting is $100, and our firm sets a target minimum return of 15 percent on all customers. Then, in order to retain

FIGURE 8.1 Comparison of Customer Selection Methods

% of Cohort		Customer Lifetime Value	Share of Wallet	RFM	Current Contribution to Profit
5	Average revenue	489,541	255,855	308,698	357,265
	Gross profit	146,862	76,766	92,609	107,719
	Variable costs	1,270	620	1,051	790
	Net profit	**145,592**	**76,146**	**91,558**	**106,389**
10	Average revenue	265,644	105,394	185,577	186,124
	Gross profit	79,699	31,618	55,667	55,837
	Variable costs	751	588	775	610
	Net profit	**78,948**	**31,030**	**54,892**	**55,227**
15	Average revenue	194,566	59,377	121,234	149,876
	Gross profit	58,370	17,813	36,370	44,963
	Variable costs	690	512	632	738
	Net profit	**57,680**	**17,301**	**35,738**	**44,225**

(Using the first 30 months of data to predict the next 18 months of purchase behavior)

Note: The reported values are in dollars and are cell medians. Gross profit is residual revenue after removing cost of goods sold. In general, for the firm that provided the database, the cost of goods sold is around 70 percent. Hence gross profit equals revenue × 0.3.
Sources: IMC International, Werner Reinartz, and V. Kumar, "Customer Relationship Characteristics on Profitable Lifetime Duration," *Journal of Marketing* 67 (January 2003), 77–99.

the customer (or sustain loyalty), our company can offer a maximum incentive of approximately $87 ($100/(1 + 15%) = $86.96). In this way, CLV_f ensures profitability without compromising loyalty.

LOYALTY TRUTH 2: CUSTOMER LOYALTY TAKES MORE TIME TO GROW THAN MOST MANAGEMENT TEAMS HAVE TO GIVE; PLANNING AND PATIENCE ARE REQUIRED

The foundation of any good loyalty initiative is information. As a result, databases are currently the vogue. But few companies today have the correct information from which to launch a proper loyalty program. And fewer still have a CEO, CIO, CMO, or other senior-level executive who has the correct vision and can convince his colleagues and board (and other stakeholders) to stay the course until the benefits of the loyalty initiative kick in.

Managers are acutely aware of the strategic benefits of customer databases. By some estimates, 95 percent of all Fortune 1000 companies either already have or are planning to create a data warehouse (a storage area for customer data to support decision making).[9] As a result, managers frequently feel that they have the situation covered when it comes to customer data, voicing a response equivalent to, "Our new Siebel (Oracle, SAP, PeopleSoft, etc.) system takes care of that." Blind reliance on off-the-shelf computer software is both an invitation for disappointment and a recipe for disaster.

Though computerized customer base systems are prevalent, rarely is it the case that firms have adequate information about their customers to effectively populate a customer base for purposes of embarking on a customer loyalty strategy. The shortage is a result of four issues:

1. *Incompatible data sources.* One of the most common problems is that customer data arrives from multiple systems that tend to have conflicting architectures, differing content, and inconsistent data formats. As Larry Ellison, CEO of Oracle, laments, "We're still trying to solve what we think is the worst problem in information processing that is preventing access to the Information Age, and that's customer data fragmentation."[10]

2. *Rapid data obsolescence.* There is the dynamic nature of customer data. Customer identities and business affiliations come and go, e-mail addresses change at a whim, and addresses and telephone numbers similarly change. Furthermore, customers' purchase histories and contact records require continual updating. There is no getting around continuous customer data management.

3. *Missing or uncollected data.* Typically, even when data is somewhat uniform and integrated, the necessary components for calculating customer CLV or prioritizing relevant, right-time

offers for customers is missing, or not in a usable format for analysis.

4. *Segregated attitudinal and behavioral data.* Most customer databases do not integrate behavioral (customer purchase) data with attitudinal (survey-based) data. This is a significant problem for developing a loyalty improvement strategy, since true customer loyalty is manifest as a combination of both attitudes and behaviors.

The requirements for an ideal customer database are listed in Figure 8.2.

But knowing what you want to do and putting processes in place is the easy part. What takes more time than most management teams are willing to give is waiting for customers and the market to understand the new approach and bring their business as a result.

FIGURE 8.2   Contents of an Ideal Customer Base

Customer Description
- Contact information
- Degree of influence in brand choice and quantity purchased

Customer's Requirements
- List of products purchased
- Share of spending for each product's category or class
- Frequency and pattern of purchasing
- Modality of purchases (how the customer places the order—in person, by telephone, etc.)

Customer's Profitability
- Number of requests for after-sales assistance
- Percentage of purchases returned for refund or exchange
- Number of logged complaints
- Average cost of servicing

Customer's Communication Preferences
- Will the customer accept sales information?
- For which categories?
- Is the customer receptive to personal sales visits?
- By what modality does the customer wish to interact?
- Are there times of the day; week; quarter or year when her time will be under severe pressure?

Source: Cartoonybin.com. Reproduced with permission.

LOYALTY TRUTH 3: FOCUS ON CUSTOMERS' SHARE-OF-WALLET. DON'T DISREGARD THOSE CUSTOMERS WITH CURRENT LOW SHARES; CUSTOMER POLYGAMY IS THE RULE THESE DAYS

Most loyalty pundits and most customer scoring methods (RFM as a prime example) are fixated on the near present, extrapolating current high purchasing activity into potential high near-future activity. Unfortunately, that is not the way nature works: Another rainstorm doesn't always follow a first; heat waves may follow one another or not. Similarly, an active customer may or may not continue her activity, depending on what share of her current spending a vendor has and what her consumption pattern looks like.

Many of the models currently employed were conceptualized in a far different marketplace from that of the early twenty-first century.

In today's world, the solitary relationships of the past have been eroded, replaced by relationships that are more polygamous. Current customers are more likely to be loyal to a group of brands than to a single brand. Consumers believe that most brands in a product category are more or less the same. As a result, consumers act in a consistent manner, by not dedicating themselves to a single brand. This is particularly true if the chosen brand is the category leader and costs more. In contrast to the "one brand for life" mentality of the past, today's consumers are blatant polygamists; rarely can a firm-customer relationship achieve monogamous exclusivity.

It's important to differentiate repeat purchasing from true loyalty. Loyalty is evoked when customers feel high involvement with products and services. Customers are willing to develop monogamous relationships in categories of importance. In situations of lower involvement, they'll fail to see the benefit of monogamous commitments. The challenge to marketers is to appreciate whatever loyalty is offered, and to strive to increase the share of requirements expended by those who are currently Desired Customers, or those who show promise of evolving into Desired Customers.

LOYALTY TRUTH 4: LOYALTY REQUIRES MUTUALLY BENEFICIAL INTERACTIONS; MOST LOYALTY PROGRAMS ARE TILTED IN THE COMPANY'S FAVOR

A compelling loyalty offering must be based on mutual benefit—a benefit for the customer as well as a benefit for the sponsoring organization. Further, rewards offered by the loyalty program must not disparage or denigrate the value of the organization's core offering. Lastly, the rewards offered must be attractive enough to impact customers' future purchasing behaviors.[11]

When loyalty programs are formulated as frequency programs, they require some unit of purchasing activity and some unit of reward to be used for banking points and for redemption. We can distinguish these units by calling the units of transaction *credits*, and the units of reward, the *currency*. Together the credits and the currency make many loyalty programs work; however, they both offer challenges for the loyalty program sponsor. Credits need to be viewed as attainable with reasonable purchase or use activity. The reason the U.S. Air Miles program failed was the tremendous activity needed to acquire and accumulate credits. If a can of a soft drink offered one credit and a six-pack 10 credits, and 15 credits were required for one airline mile (the currency), it seemed hardly worth the effort. Customers could not imagine being able to accumulate enough credits to make participation worthwhile.

The currency of loyalty programs is how activity is ultimately rewarded. It is the attraction of the frequency program. We believe that too many companies look outside their own domain for a loyalty currency. This is a mistake. For example, a European telephone company was building a frequency program and was planning on using airline miles as its currency! It had the opportunity to create loyalty currency within its own operations, but yielded to what it saw being used in the marketplace. Not only were airline miles re-

Source: Cartoonybin.com. Reproduced with permission.

moved from its product domain, they were also expensive for it to purchase, while its own product, telephone minutes of usage, was practically free.

LOYALTY TRUTH 5: THE CHAIN OF EVENTS FROM LOYALTY TO PROFITS IS TWISTED AND COMPLEX. LEARN THE SPECIFIC RESPONSE PATTERNS OF YOUR CUSTOMERS IN YOUR INDUSTRY

There are no surrogates for understanding how your own customers will behave. The chain of events from loyalty to profitability is far from straightforward. To make it work for you, you must understand your unique customers and situation. Simply applying conventional wisdom is courting financial disaster.

The authors have previously popularized the notion of the asymmetric, nonlinear relationships that exist up and down the Performance-Satisfaction-Retention-Profit Chain.[12] As companies look to monitor the ROI on their loyalty initiatives, it is critical that they understand the way in which investments (in processes and programs) manifest in outputs for the individual company. This means creating a response function that accurately portrays the responses for the organization's own customers in its particular industry.[13]

LOYALTY TRUTH 6: SATISFIED AND LOYAL EMPLOYEES CAN MAKE A DIFFERENCE, BUT CUSTOMER SATISFACTION AND LOYALTY CAN AND OFTEN DOES HAPPEN IN THE ABSENCE OF EMPLOYEE SATISFACTION AND LOYALTY

The history of sports is replete with stories of all-star, highly talented teams that have gone down to defeat at the hands of tightly knit bands of relatively unknown underdogs. Such events often become the stuff of sporting legend, but they have their analogs in the triumphs of the business world as well. However, the equivalence is not directly related to a business as a team of employees, so much as it is the proper implementation of a total game plan by a committed coaching staff who understand the interplay of the team's personnel with the goal to be attained.

A simplistic approach to employees' contributions to customer loyalty preaches achieving high morale, invoking dedication, and rewarding good performance. This is why so many loyalty programs initiated with the corps of employees are doomed to failure. While employees make critical contributions, they are not the critical key, and their morale is not as important to success as many would have us believe. What matters is how well a business equips its employees to accomplish a task that they fully understand. We have referred to this as the service climate in which employees work, which is most closely related to customers' loyalty. Professor Benjamin Schneider defines service climate as "The degree to which the company has in place policies, practices and procedures, and ways of rewarding, support-

To the dismay of most authors, customers really did judge a book by its cover.

Source: Cartoonybin.com. Reproduced with permission.

ing, and expecting the kinds of behavior that yield quality and customer satisfaction."[14]

LOYALTY TRUTH 7: CUSTOMER LOYALTY AND BRAND IMAGERY ARE FAR FROM INDEPENDENT; YOU MUST MANAGE THEM HAND-IN-HAND

While admittedly observational in nature, it can be argued that marketing as a science has largely focused on brand-centric objectives. (This preoccupation has only recently been challenged by the popularization of customer-centric agendas introduced by customer satisfaction audits and customer needs/requirements studies.) Simplistically, brand-centric marketing can be thought of as manipulating the elements of the marketing mix (commonly referred to as the "Four Ps": product, price, promotion, and place) to improve the status or health of a brand (a condition commonly summarized in the concept of "brand equity"). The ultimate goal of such efforts is to enhance the bundle of benefits offered by a firm's product or service in comparison to competing alternatives. As the firm's offer surpasses competition, it is assumed market share will follow.

In contrast, customer-centric marketing (the newer perspective) largely focuses on efforts to improve customers' perceptions of their experiences in using an organization's products or services, and in relating to the organization itself. Customer-centric strategies tend to focus on improving customers' levels of satisfaction with the product and with the customer experience. The goal of these efforts is to lengthen customer lifetimes and to increase customers' lifetime profits through increased spending.[15] In opposition to brand-centric marketing's focus on attracting more customers (conquest marketing), customer-centric marketing is aimed largely at reducing customer defection and strengthening current customers' loyalty (retention marketing).

While both brand-centric and customer-centric approaches are ultimately aimed at manipulating customers' attitudes and behaviors, managers and researchers tend to isolate these functions. For example, in most firms, brand management efforts are usually considered separately from satisfaction management efforts, and are frequently the responsibilities of different departments within the organization. Similarly, specialized scholarly journals have evolved for researchers dedicated to the focus of either brand-specific or customer-specific issues. We believe it is time for businesses to adopt a holistic approach by combining the power of the brand with the power of the customer.

This approach has been given a voice in a recent theory in which the personal identification of a customer with a brand is differentiated from a customer's relationship with the brand's manufacturer. In their book *Driving Customer Equity*, researchers Rust, Zeithaml, and Lemon define the new construct of customer equity by incorporating both brand-centric and customer-centric marketing activities.[16] Customer equity, according to Rust et al., includes:

- *Value equity*—the customer's objective assessment of the utility of a brand. This assessment is driven by the product's quality, price, and convenience.

- *Brand equity*—the customer's subjective and intangible assessment of the brand built through image and meaning. This assessment is influenced by brand awareness, the consumer's attitude toward the brand, and the firm's corporate citizenship.

- *Relationship equity*—a subjective predisposition to stay with a brand because of its familiarity, difficulties of switching, or a trust in the brand's sales staff.

The components of customer equity are key drivers of a firm's efforts to improve customers' CLV_j. But as they span both conquest and retention marketing efforts, they require an integrated, singularly managed approach.

BUILDING A LOYALTY PROCESS

Having identified so many of the foibles of current loyalty marketing practice, it's time to suggest a better way. We believe appropriate loyalty programs ought to be designed according to the five-step process shown in Figure 8.3. The five steps are as follows:

1. *Observation.* This is a stage of accumulating all information possible about customers from many disparate and often siloed sources, including:

- ▌ Purchase records and history.
- ▌ Costs associated with servicing each customer.
- ▌ Demographic information.
- ▌ The share-of-wallet or of spending that each customer gives us.

2. *Scoring.* By weighting purchase expectations with size of purchase and costs of servicing, we arrive at what we call an "inertial customer lifetime value"—the potential lifetime value were we to take no action to nurture or to fire the customer.

3. *Selection.* With scores completed for each of our customers, we are in position to segment them into the three categories we discussed in the Introduction: Desired Customers, Break-even Customers, and Costly Customers.

4. *Prioritization.* We divide each of these three customer groups into pairs—low share-of-spending and high share-of-spending. Then we determine which customers to focus developmental efforts on. Our key metric is share of current spending. Our process allows for six implementation strategies:

1. Improving our financial gains from low-share Costly Customers by reducing our costs of servicing them, moving them to the status of low-share Break-even Customers.

2. Improving our financial gains from low-share Costly Customers by both increasing their share-of-spending and controlling the costs of servicing them, advancing them to high-share Break-even Customers.

3. Improving our financial gains from low-share Break-even Customers by controlling our offers to them and, where possible, reducing our costs of servicing them, moving them to low-share Desired Customers.

FIGURE 8.3 A Loyalty Process Model

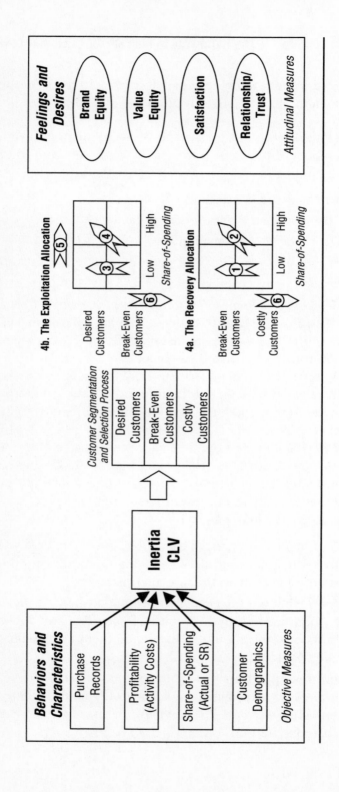

4. Improving our financial gains from low-share Break-even Customers by increasing their share-of-spending and by controlling the costs of servicing them, advancing them to high-share Desired Customers.

5. Improving our financial gains from low-share Desired Customers by increasing their share of spending, evolving them into high-share Desired Customers.

6. Divesting ourselves of low-share Costly Customers and low-share Break-even Customers whose purchasing behavior cannot be improved.

The value of each of the first five strategies can be tested by computing the ROI corresponding to each level of transformation. The change strategy yielding the greatest positive, surplus ROI will be the first to be pursued.

5. *Leveraging.* Though the logic of the five improvement strategies is obvious and builds on the work of Reinartz and Kumar, and of Rust, Zeithaml, and Lemon, we add an action component: how to leverage aspects of the customer and brand experience to grow the selected customers as we would wish them to grow. The four tools for this growth are brand equity, value equity, relationship equity, and satisfaction.

IMPLEMENTING THE LOYALTY PROCESS

Now let's look at each stage of the loyalty process in greater detail.

Step 1: Observation

The first stage, *observation*, is the objective stage. We've listed four critical components of information that need to be collected. Too often this information will exist in incompatible formats in databases of radically different architecture. Hopefully a uniform "key" (customer identifier) will exist in all databases that can be used to merge the data at the level of the individual customer.

Focusing on actual, disaggregated customer data, as we prefer to do, we choose a arbitrary time period for analysis of spending and customer value. The choice of this time period has to take into account the purchasing patterns dictated by the product or service category, so the time period cannot be arbitrarily chosen. For skis it could be 36 months, or 12 quarters. For automobiles it would be longer, at least 40 months for leases and 5 to 10 years for purchased vehicles.

While four groups of measures are listed, other information can also be incorporated. The most critical component is a measure of the customer's worth to the enterprise: *purchasing activity*. Within the time period of analysis, all purchases must be trackable in terms of their size and their pattern. This information will become the basis for event history modeling, a process used successfully by Reinartz and Kumar in their study of spending and customer loyalty.[17] But too many customer loyalty analyses have been flawed by using revenue rather than profit data, so we recommend that a second component also be gathered or estimated: *activity costs*, the costs of servicing each customer. This information should cover the same time period. It will indicate what activities the organization had to conduct in order to receive each customer's purchases.

The third essential component is *share-of-spending* information. Ideally this can be obtained through third-party clearing houses. In many industries, certain research firms interview major customers or audit their expenditures to report the relative share enjoyed by each major product vendor. In other cases, the customer will willingly report his total capital budget for a category (from which share figures can be determined) or will estimate the share of his spending being allocated to a firm. Without the benefit of share data, increases in spending will always look impressive.

Finally, *customer demographics* (or, in B2B settings, what we call "firmographics" or "industrographics") provide a useful adjunct to the activity information of the first three components. This information can assist in revealing customer clustering, which might otherwise be overlooked. It can also provide useful covariates for advanced statistical analyses. See Figure 8.4 for a list of possible information to be compiled about customers.

FIGURE 8.4 Useful Demographics Information

For B2B Customers
- Customer's years in business
- Customer's gross revenue
- Number of locations a customer has
- Customer's Dun & Bradstreet rating
- Customer's decision-making process: centralized/decentralized
- Number of executives involved in customer's decision-making unit
- How we interact with customer: impersonally/personally
- Number of competitors with whom customer does business
- Customer's complaint/returns activity

For B2C Customers
- Customer's age
- Customer's household income
- Customer's household size
- Customer's activity (has he/she contacted our customer service center? complained? complimented? given us a referral?)
- Customer's receptivity to deals/offers
- Customer's geodemographic code (PRIZM®; ACORN™; MOSAIC™, etc.)
- Customer's credit rating

Step 2: Calculating Inertial CLV_f

Determining contribution to profit from each customer (projected purchases minus anticipated costs of servicing), we produce an inertial CLV_f. We call it inertial because the figure represents the current status. It provides a convenient metric by which we can segment customers for the next step. But we are not so shortsighted as to imply that this CLV_f is the best that each customer can do for us. We use the metric simply for intermediate classification purposes. We're all about using loyalty to develop stronger relationships.

Step 3: Selection

Using the inertial CLV_f, customers can be allocated to one of the three customer types we've previously described: Desired Customers, Break-even Customers, and Costly Customers. The allocation is obvious, but the message from this step is profound. We believe very few businesses will have audited their customer relationships in this way. The proportion of customers in each of the three categories reveals much about the health of the current business and the astuteness by which the enterprise has managed its customer relationships. Having more than 15 percent of customers in the "Costly Customer" category is likely indicative of a bad situation, especially if any of these have previously been touted as good customers, or if any of these customers are major revenue producers.

Step 4: Prioritization

This is the step where the rubber meets the road. It is here that hard choices about specific customers need to be made. Decisions made here become the raison d'etre of all future loyalty initiatives. The enterprise should first complete the scorecard shown in Figure 8.5. Answers to the questions in the scorecard help direct priorities for the proper use of customer loyalty.

Each strategy of the Prioritization phase depicted in Figure 8.3 directs action toward a specific segment of customers as the focus of loyalty efforts. How to approach loyalty is covered in the last step.

Step 5: Leveraging

Each strategy requires moving as many customers as possible from one status to another. The mechanism for accomplishing this shift will be one of the four tools listed under "Feelings and Desires" in Figure 8.3. Though it might be ideal to court each customer within the chosen segment with the tool most resonant for him, at this stage we must adopt a general theme for the loyalty program. Consequently, we need to assess which of the four will offer the most leverage in moving customers in the direction suggested by the strategy.

The tools are listed in approximate hierarchical order. That is, the status of the brand, *brand equity*, is predominant. Next most im-

FIGURE 8.5   The Customer Base Scorecard

Step	Customers	Condition	Action (Refers to Loyalty Process, Figure 8.3, Prioritization column)
1.	What percent of customers are Costly Customers? _____	Is the proportion of Costly Customers equal to or greater than 15 percent?	If so, work from matrix 4a, the Recovery Allocation. Strategies 1 and 2 apply.
		If less than 15 percent go to Step 2.	
2.	What percent of customers are Break-even Customers? _____	Is the proportion of Break-even Customers greater than the proportion of Desired Customers?	If so, work from matrix 4b, the Exploitation Allocation. Strategies 3 and 4 apply.
		If less, go to Step 3.	
3.	What percent of customers are Desired Customers? _____	Desired Customers represent the majority of your customers.	If so, work from matrix 4b, the Exploitation Allocation. Strategy 5 applies.
4.	Examine your Costly Customers	Determine which ones you should stop servicing.	Use Strategy 6 in matrices 4a and 4b.

portant is *value equity,* followed by *satisfaction* and *relationship equity.* The hierarchy offers a mandate to utilize those tools that are predominant rather than arbitrarily choosing a tool. To select a tool, the organization will require survey data from a sample of customers in the chosen segment. Their attitudes (on as many of the tools as possible) will help to determine where the greatest deficit occurs. The appropriate inventories of customers' attitudes are indicated by the lists in Figure 8.6. Identified deficits must be capable of being

FIGURE 8.6 Components of the Leveraging Tools

Brand Equity
■ Awareness/Salience of the Brand
  ■ *Communications mix*—the customer's perception of the brand's combination of advertising, sales promotion, public relations, and personal selling. How compatible and successful is the brand's media mix in communicating with present customers?
  ■ *Media*—the specific media vehicles employed by the brand. How compatible and successful are the vehicles to the customer's lifestyle and media preferences/habits?
  ■ *Message*—the brand's core message that it seeks to communicate initially.
■ Attitudes toward the Brand
  ■ *Communications message*—the ongoing communication or empathy created by the logical and emotional message.
  ■ *Special events*—how customers can develop personal associations with the brand beyond the use experience (as through NASCAR sponsorships, Jeep Jamborees, sponsored concerts, etc.).
  ■ *Brand extensions (family)*—customers' perceptions of the coherency and integrity of the brand family.
  ■ *Brand partners*—the extent to which customers perceive that alignments and partnerships with other brands are positive or negative.
  ■ *Product placement and celebrity endorsements*—customers' takeaway from products and services being seen in movies and TV shows and through celebrities endorsing the products.
■ Citizenship/Ethics of the Brand
  ■ *Community events*—participation in the customer's local community.
  ■ *Privacy policies*—customers' understanding of and satisfaction with the way the firm retains information about them.
  ■ *Environmental record*—is the firm perceived as a friend of the environment?
  ■ *Hiring and employee practices*—is the firm perceived as being a fair and open employer?
  ■ *Guarantees and service obligations*—how well the firm is perceived to stand behind the quality and functionality of its products and services.

Value Equity
■ Quality
  ■ Quality of the physical product or of the service product.
  ■ Quality of the delivery component—the processes by which organizations respond to their customers' expectations.
  ■ Quality of the accompanying servicing.
■ Price
  ■ The basic, everyday price.
  ■ Offered discounts and sales.
  ■ Payment plans and terms.

FIGURE 8.6 *(Continued)*

- Convenience
  - Location—physical location or accessibility.
  - Ease of use.
  - Availability—hours and days of operation, speed of contact.

Relationship Equity

- Loyalty programs—the positive or negative contribution a loyalty or frequency program may convey to the firm.
- Recognition and appreciation programs—the extent to which participating customers can and do feel rewarded.
- Affinity programs—what other nonmonetary opportunities are there for customers to increase their emotional attachment to the firm?
- Customer communities—does the brand or firm offer a focus around which customers are willing to organize, as with the Harley-Davidson Owners Groups (HOGS)?
- Knowledge building programs—the extent to which the firm is perceived to engage in a learning relationship with customers, such that the customer's status and ease of doing business is enhanced.

Satisfaction*

- Product/Service Key Driver 1
- Product/Service Key Driver 2
- Product/Service Key Driver 3
- Product/Service Key Driver n

---

*The Key Drivers will vary by product and service. They cannot be anticipated but must be determined on an individual product-by-product, service-by-service basis through empirical data (of the sort usually collected in customer satisfaction surveys).
Source: Adapted from Roland T. Rust, Valerie A. Zeithaml, and Katherine N. Lemon, *Driving Customer Equity* (New York: The Free Press, 2004).

remedied; otherwise they offer little or no opportunity. The organization must cautiously and realistically evaluate its ability to close any discovered gaps.

We make the assumption that as we remedy these gaps, deficit customers will be more likely to commit more of their business to the enterprise, thereby accomplishing the goal of the strategy being

FIGURE 8.7 Strategy Worksheet

	Attitude Scores			
	Col A	Col B	Col C	Col D
	Our Brand	Highest Scoring Competitor	Difference (Columns A and B)	Rank Tools by Differences
Brand Equity				
Value Equity				
Satisfaction				
Relationship Equity				

pursued. The Strategy Worksheet in Figure 8.7 outlines the process more completely.

To select among the tools, a pro forma ROI can be calculated for each tool. An assumed "take" (on the part of customers) will have to be used to calculate the impact of the tool on greater spending and consequently an improved CLV_f. The four tools can then be rank-ordered according to the potential impact from improvements on each.

FROM THE CUSTOMER'S PERSPECTIVE

Our review of customer loyalty has highlighted some of the inappropriate actions of businesses, and has offered suggestions on how businesses can treat their customers better. The authors believe that a business managed with its customers' benefit in mind can be a winning situation for everyone involved, especially the customer. We hope most businesses come to view the marketplace in this manner. But until then, what can customers themselves do to benefit from

Gargantuan Insurance

Customer Acquisition Process

Customer Retention Process

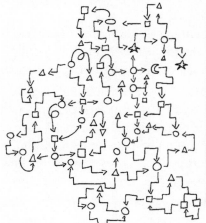

Send Holiday Card

Source: Cartoonybin.com. Reproduced with permission.

good loyalty programs and to avoid poor loyalty programs? Here are 11 suggestions:

1. Stay informed. Know your rights as a consumer when consenting to participate in any loyalty program, and rigorously defend these rights.

2. Avoid the sunk-cost fallacy of remaining loyal to a company that dissatisfies you simply because you have accumulated points toward some rewards, especially when you need a lot more points before you can redeem them for any reward. (This sunk-cost trap can probably also be applied to other business relationships where procrastination delays switching—besides the context of loyalty programs)

3. Read the company's privacy statement before consenting to provide personal information, and ask how the company plans to use the information. If the uses include benefits you're interested in, comply; otherwise, refuse.

4. Only provide your personal information to a company you believe will reward you with relevant and valuable offers. If you are dissatisfied with the way a company uses your information, report this to the company and request that you be taken off its mailing lists.

5. Inform company management of service problems or other dissatisfactions. Communicate your concerns to local personnel first, but escalate your complaints to corporate management if they're not resolved by local management.

6. If an organization doesn't address your complaints satisfactorily, don't go back—ever. Vote with your feet! Companies typically believe that customers will endure substantial inconveniences and disappointments, so they have little incentive to change—particularly when customers do return.

7. If a problem with a firm is serious, lodge complaints with organizations such as the Better Business Bureau. No firm wants a pattern of complaints logged against it with such organizations.

8. Recognize that if you appreciate good service, it may cost you a little more. Your dollars are votes, so if you continue to reelect bad companies by allocating your dollars to them, then you will continue to get bad service.

9. Don't conduct business with unpleasant companies with poor or nonexistent service, even if their products are acceptable. Look for an alternative supplier offering both good products and good, friendly service.

10. Escalate praise as easily as you escalate a complaint. Star performers need to know their efforts are appreciated. Letters provide short-term feedback more quickly than your eventual repurchase.

11. Tell friends and associates about good and bad companies, especially when asked, but even when not asked, if you feel strongly enough about the organization.

If we, as consumers, wish to live in a kinder, gentler world, then we have a responsibility to act in a way that fosters this. Businesses act in their self-interest. If the market demands better service (meaning customers will pay for it) then they will answer that need. But if they are not given that message, they will continue in their current behavior, assuming that consumers are complacent and willing to suffer the current conditions. In short, it's up to customers to lead large organizations in the direction that will serve them both.

SETTING THE RECORD STRAIGHT: THE RIGHT WAY TO MANAGE FOR CUSTOMER LOYALTY

In this chapter we have offered what we believe to be the most reasonable approach to constructing a customer loyalty program that is directed at the greatest opportunities for an enterprise. In contrast, most other loyalty programs today are one-size-fits-all Band-Aids that fail to acknowledge the idiosyncrasies of a business, and then compound this oversight by treating all of the business's customers the same.

Contrary to the common lament, customer loyalty is *not* dead. Unfortunately, neither are badly managed loyalty initiatives by companies. As Tansaş CEO Servet Topaloğlu observed, you have to give the customer a reason for him to believe your firm deserves his loyalty.

It is also important to remember that firms operate now in one of the most competitive markets in history. This means that offers and actions that once delighted customers will one day become what customers expect. Such is the demanding nature of competition.

Similarly, the tools to enhance customer loyalty will continue to evolve, just as customers' expectations of what organizations should do to deserve their loyalty will change. We trust our readers will remain open to evolving approaches and will stay mindful of the obligation to monitor customers' behavior as the result of each new loyalty endeavor. Such fact-finding becomes critical when upper management begins asking tough questions about the apparent unresponsiveness of a brand's customer franchise to a loyalty program. It's defensive, but it's also just good, plain, common sense to track what a company gets back from its loyalty initiatives. Our view is that each dollar appropriately invested in nurturing customer loyalty will pay substantial rewards in the future, but managers require that this view be proven with factual results.

We end this book as we began it. Our goal is to dispel the myths of loyalty so that businesses can effectively leverage customer loyalty to help them survive and succeed. In this way we can all win—by being good to one another.

ACKNOWLEDGMENTS

As authors Keiningham, Vavra, and Aksoy reflect on the circumstances that brought us together and the way events have unfolded, we are convinced of the guidance of a Divine Hand. Therefore, we wish to begin by giving thanks to God for bringing us together and for the many blessings in our lives.

We want first to thank those men and women who pioneered the loyalty movement, alerting the business community to the folly of chasing elusive potential customers while, for the most part, disregarding those who were already customers. A primary spokesperson for this movement has been Frederick Reichheld, to whom we all owe a considerable debt. While not all of these pioneers' initial observations have passed rigorous subsequent investigation, their energy for the message

Source: Cartoonybin.com. Reproduced with permission.

created an awareness that would not otherwise have occurred. We also acknowledge that many of our own initial ideas regarding customer loyalty have similarly been shown to be oversimplifications. But the contribution of these pioneers far exceeds the errors, and we are in their debt.

It is impossible to name all the people who provided support in the writing of this book. There are, however, several individuals and companies who were invaluable to its completion.

We are particularly grateful to our wonderful literary agents, Michael Ebeling and Ana Hayes of Ebeling-Hayes. Thank you for sharing our vision and, more importantly, for being wonderful people. We are also indebted to Joel Roberts of Joel D. Roberts and Associates—without question, you are the best media trainer/consultant on the planet, and our writing greatly benefited from working with you. We also recognize the contribution to this project made by Jane Wesman, Andrea Stein, and Lori Ames of Jane Wesman Public Relations. Putting a vision in writing is one thing, but gaining it voice and recognition in today's overly crowded media requires the knowledge, expertise, and practice of skilled public relations professionals. You are true professionals. Thank you!

A special thanks is owed to Lawrence Alexander and Matthew Holt of John Wiley and Sons for believing in and supporting *Loyalty Myths*. Without this commitment to publishing our ideas, *Loyalty Myths* would be little more than a message in a bottle.

We are grateful to Linda Indig of John Wiley and Sons, the staff at Cape Cod Compositors, and Erin Williams of Indent Publishing Services, whose comments on style and substance helped to transform our manuscript into something far more readable than we could have accomplished on our own.

We are also thankful to have been able to team with Katrin Keiningham of Cartoonybin.com to produce the cartoons that are dispersed throughout this book. Our desire was to make *Loyalty Myths* as fun as possible, and to make certain that we did not take ourselves too seriously. The cartoons greatly help us in achieving that objective.

We are especially thankful to all the clients of Ipsos Loyalty, whose partnership has shaped our thinking and enriched our lives. We wish to thank all of our colleagues at Ipsos Loyalty and KOÇ University, whose talent, imagination, and dedication are a fountain of inspiration. We especially want to thank Elaine Chang, Sharan Duggal, Andi Jenkins, Catherine Martell, Gailynn Nicks, Kenneth Peterson, Doug Pruden, Brenda Rivera, Brian Sattin, and Pierre Turrene of Ipsos Loyalty for their review and contributions to a series of drafts as this book took shape, which greatly aided in the quality of the final manuscript.

We end by giving the greatest thanks to our families, who have endured the unrewarding task of having to provide emotional support and encouragement while we spent many long nights squirreled away writing and unable to reciprocate. Michiko, Hana, and Sage Keiningham; Linda and Kerry Vavra, Stacy Roux, and Tammy Collins; Ihsan, and Levent Aksoy; Pelin and Miray Kurtay: thank you for your love, patience, and understanding—and, most importantly, for allowing us to follow our calling.

Terry Vavra dedicates his role in the writing of this book to his mother, Gwen C. Vavra (Filipy). He acknowledges the enthusiasm for life and the optimistic outlook that she taught him. In many ways, his current position and capacity to co-write this book was a result of her countless bedtime readings of Watty Piper's *The Little Train that Could*. Having lost her husband and Terry's father in 1977, she reinvented herself as a realtor, living and making new friends across the West Coast. Now, as Terry finishes his part of this project, Gwen at 91 years of age is challenged with amyotrophic lateral sclerosis (ALS). But she hasn't given up—she continues to enjoy herself and life and has never lost her wonderful sense of humor. She sets a wonderful role model for Terry and his (and Linda's) three daughters. "Thanks, Mom, for everything!"

On his behalf, Henri Wallard would like to add the following: Many books have been written about customer loyalty. It is a field with rapidly shifting parameters given the evolution of customer information systems, survey methodologies, and computer analytic capacities: unimaginable 15 years ago. Any rapid inflation of information can lead to confusion, and our hope is that this book will contribute to clarifying the issues regarding customer loyalty and customer relationship management (CRM).

Writing *Loyalty Myths* has been an exciting adventure. Many people have contributed to the achievement of this project and my understanding. I am very grateful to Jean-Marc Lech and Didier Truchot for

Source: Cartoonybin.com. Reproduced with permission.

their active support regarding publications, and for their help in the development of this book. I am also indebted to the Ipsos Loyalty team, whose enthusiasm and imagination have greatly enhanced my own understanding. I wish in particular to express my gratitude to Gailynn Nicks, Mustapha Tabba, Steve Levy, Tom Neri, Alain Peron, Antoine Moreau, Antoine Solom, Jose Roberto Labinas, Ignacio Lavallen, Carolina Gerenzani, Sundip Chahal, Catherine Martell, Carlos Harding, and Pascal Bourgeat.

I want to recognize and thank V. Kumar and Roland Rust for their ideas and leadership with regard to the final chapter of the book. Lastly, I want to thank my coauthors with whom this book was created, Lerzan Aksoy, Terry Vavra, and Timothy Keiningham.

NOTES

PREFACE

1. Quoted in Arthur Marx, *Goldwyn: A Biography of the Man Behind the Myth* (New York: Ballantine Books, 1977), chap. 27.
2. Michael D. Lemonick, "Hawking Cries Uncle," *Time*, (August 2, 2004), p. 65.
3. Quoted in Philipp Frank, *Einstein, His Life and Times* (George Rosen, translator) (New York: Da Capo Press, 2002).
4. Mark Twain (Samuel Langhorne Clemens), "Consistency," a paper read in Hartford, Connecticut, 1884; reprinted in Charles Neider, ed., *The Complete Essays of Mark Twain* (New York: Da Capo Press, 2000).

INTRODUCTION   The Myths of Loyalty: Did the Gods Mislead Us?

1. Frederick F. Reichheld, *Loyalty Rules* (Boston: Harvard Business School Press, 1990).
2. Melvin Thomas Copeland, "Relation of Consumer's Buying Habits to Marketing Methods," *Harvard Business Review* 1, no. 1 (April, 1923), 282–289.
3. Reichheld, Frederick F., and W. Earl Sasser, Jr. (1990), "Zero Defections: Quality Comes to Services," *Harvard Business Review* 68, no. 5, pp. 105–111.
4. The Conference Board, *The CEO Challenge: Top Marketplace and Management Issues—2002*, New York.
5. META Group, "Industry Overview: New Insights in Data Warehousing Solutions," *Information Week*, 1996, 1–27HP.
6. Susannah Patton, "The Truth about CRM," *CIO* 14, no. 14 (May 1, 2001), 77.
7. Ibid.
8. Ibid.
9. Arthur Middleton Hughes, "A Failing Grade," *Target Marketing* 26, no. 11 (November, 2003), 51–53, 72.
10. Arthur Middleton Hughes, "Editorial: The Mirage of CRM," *Journal of Database Management* 9, no. 2 (January, 2002), 102–104.
11. John McKenzie, "Serving Suggestions," *Financial Management*, December 2001, 26–27.
12. Patton, "The Truth about CRM."
13. Food Marketing Institute, "New Directions in Advertising: Marketing the Retail Store as a Brand," April 22, 2002.
14. James Cigiliano, Margaret Georgiadis, Darren Pleasance, and Susan Whalley, "The Price of Loyalty," *McKinsey Quarterly*, Issue 4, 2000.

15. Web Flyer, "2002 Membership Numbers in Frequent Travel Programmes," www.webflyer.com, December 5, 2004.
16. "Loyalty Trends for the 21st Century," *Credit Card Management* 17, no. 10 (December 2004), 39.
17. Emma Warrillow & Associates "The Impact of Loyalty Programmes on the Buying Behaviours of Small Business Owners," EmmaWarrillow.com, November 21, 2004.
18. Michael T. Capezzi, Rick Ferguson, and Richard Cuthbertson, "Loyalty Trends for the 21st Century," *Journal of Targeting, Measurement and Analysis for Marketing* 12, no. 3 (March 2004), 199–212.
19. Ibid.
20. Ibid.
21. Quadstone, "Savvy Consumers Understand Trade-Off between Personal Data and Better Service," press release, August 27, 2001.
22. Michael T. Capezzi and Rick Ferguson, *Trendtalk: Loyalty Trends for the 21st Century*, report by the Colloquy Group, no. 6.03 (July 2003).
23. Cigiliano, et al, "The Price of Loyalty."
24. Phil Clarke, "One for All," *Best's Review*, April 2004, 43–45.
25. Lior Arussy, "Don't Take Calls, Make Contact," *Harvard Business Review*, January 2002, 16–17.
26. Jon Anton, "The Past, Present and Future of Customer Access Centers," *International Journal of Service Industry Management*, vol. 11, no. 2, (2000) 120–130.
27. Bharat Kumar, "Go for Gold," *Businessline*, December 3, 2003, 1.
28. Colin Armistead, Julia Kiely, Linda Hole, and Jean Prescott, "An Exploration of Managerial Issues in Call Centres," *Managing Service Quality* 12, no. 4 (2002) 246–256.
29. Noah Gans, Ger Koole, and Avishai Mandelbaum, "Telephone Call Centers: Tutorial, Review, and Research Prospects," *Manufacturing & Service Operations Management* 5, no. 2 (Spring 2000), 79–141.
30. Peter Lewis, "So Much For Customer Service," *Fortune*, August 28, 2003, http://www.fortune.com/fortune/subs/columnist/0,15704,479455,00.html.
31. Mary Hayes, "Delta Looks Offshore to Save Money: Call-center services in India and the Philippines save the airline $26 million," *Information Week*, June 23, 2003.
32. Harry R. Weber, "Delta to Close India Call Center," *AP Online*, July 28, 2004.
33. Kevin J. Clancy, "Save America's Dying Brands," *Marketing Management* 10, no. 3 (September/October 2001), 36–41.
34. Matthew Boyle, "Brand Killers," *Fortune*, 148, no. 3 (August 11, 2003), 89.
35. Cigiliano, et al, "The Price of Loyalty."

CHAPTER 1   Loyalty Myths That Subvert Company Goals

1. *Fair Disclosure Wire*, "Q1 2004 Nextel Partners Earnings Conference Call—Final," April 28, 2004.
2. Frederick F. Reichheld, and David W. Kenny, "The Hidden Advantages of Customer Retention," *Journal of Retail Banking* 12, no. 4 (Winter 1990–1991), 19–23.

3. Quality Focus Institute Staff, "Deciding Where to Start on Service Quality," *Bank Marketing*, April 1991, 50–52.
4. Maria Mooshil, and Beth Healy, "At First Chicago, Fees, Fie, Foes . . . Fumble," *Crain's Chicago Business* 18, no. 19 (May 8, 1995), 3.
5. Ibid.
6. Russell Mitchell, and Richard A. Melcher, "Thanks for Your Deposit. That'll Be $3," *Business Week*, May 15, 1995, 46.
7. Reported in George M. Morvis, "Avoiding a 'Fee'-asco," *Retail Banking Digest* 15, no. 3 (May/June 1995), 12.
8. Carla Fried, "Fees from Hell: How Fiendish Is Your Bank?" *Money*, July 1995, 44.
9. Barry Meier, "Need a Teller? A Big Bank Plans $3 Fee," *New York Times*, April 27, 1995, D1.
10. Reported in Dan Clark, "The Winds of Change Blow Hard against Chicago's First National," *Credit Union News* 15, no. 14 (July 28, 1995), 7.
11. Virginia Dean, "In Defense of Mistakes," *Banker News* 5, no. 24 (Dec 2, 1997), 6.
12. Olaf de Senerpont Domis, "Teller Fee Spurs Call for Boycott of First Chicago," *American Banker*, May 4, 1995, 2.
13. R. Christian Bruce, "Waters, Kennedy Protest Bank Fees, Pledge Push for Basic Banking Bill," *BNA's Banking Report* 64, no. 19 (May 8, 1995), 896.
14. *Journal Record (Oklahoma City, OK)* "Chicago Banks Have Field Day on Rival's New Teller Fee Plan," May 5, 1995.
15. Phil Britt, "First Chicago Decision Starts Marketing Wave," *America's Community Banker* 4, no. 7 (July 1995), 10.
16. Barbara F. Bronstien, "Marketing: Small Banks Have a Blast with 1st Chicago Teller Fees," *American Banker* 160, no. 88 (May 9, 1995), 8.
17. Jeffrey Noe, "Regaining Customer Appreciation," *America's Community Banker* 5, no. 4 (April 1996), 16.
18. *Journal Record*, "Chicago Banks Have Field Day."
19. Barbara Bronstien, "In Chicago Flap over Fees, the Data Support Smaller Banks," *American Banker*, August 4, 1995, 7.
20. John W. Milligan, "Banking's Loyalty Problem," *US Banker* 105, no. 10 (October 1995), 39–42.
21. FDIC data, October 5, 2004 http://www2.fdic.gov/sod/sodMarketBank.asp?barItem=2.
22. *Financial Services Report (Potomac)* (1995), "All Eyes Are on First Chicago's Teller Fees," (May 24), 1.
23. Reichheld and Kenny, "The Hidden Advantages of Customer Retention."
24. Brett Chase, "First Chicago NBD to Cut Its Controversial Teller Fee on Most Accounts," *American Banker* 161, no. 68 (April 10, 1996), 4.
25. Orla O'Sullivan, "Some of Your Customers Are Unprofitable. OK, Now What?" *ABA Banking Journal* 89, no. 11 (November 1997), 42–46, 93.
26. Marion R. Foote, "First Chicago's Account Realignment Succeeds," *Journal of Retail Banking Services* 18, no. 1 (Spring 1996), 21.

27. Timothy L. Keiningham, and Terry G. Vavra, *The Customer Delight Principle: Exceeding Customers' Expectations for Bottom-Line Success* (New York: McGraw-Hill, 2002), 11.

28. Theodore Levitt, "Marketing Myopia," *Harvard Business Review* 38 (July–August 1960), 26–44, 173–181.

29. Bob Shallit, "Broke But Beloved," Bob Shallit Column, *The Sacramento Bee*, May 27, 2002.

30. Judy Wells, and Earl Daniels, "Loyal Following Couldn't Keep Jacksonville, Mich.–Based Jacobson's Going," *The Florida Times-Union*, July 27, 2002.

31. *Business Wire*, "Garden Botanika Makes Chapter 11 Bankruptcy Filing With $7.0 Million in Debtor-in-Possession Financing; Store Closings to be a Part of Reorganization Effort," April 20, 1999.

32. Philip Kotler, *Marketing Management: Analysis, Planning, Implementation and Control*, 9th edition (Upper Saddle River, NJ: Prentice Hall, 1997).

33. *Seattle Post-Intelligencer*, "Steve Jobs Retakes Control: Hesitant Co-founder Will Run Apple until a New CEO Is Found," August 8, 1997.

34. Pui-Yan Lam, "May the Force of the Operating System Be with You: Macintosh Devotion as Implicit Religion," *Sociology of Religion*, June 22, 2001.

35. Neha Kaushik, "The Promise in Promotions: Promotions, Whose Need Is Increasingly Being Felt by the Surging Services Sector, Will Click if They Realise Marketing Objectives and Reinforce Brand Values," *Businessline*, September 4, 2003.

36. Jeff Zabin, and Gresh Brebach, *Precision Marketing: The New Rules for Attracting, Retaining, and Leveraging Profitable Customers* (New York: John Wiley & Sons, 2004).

37. Timothy L. Keiningham, Lerzan Aksoy, Tiffany Perkins-Munn, and Terry G. Vavra, "The Convergence of Brand-Centric and Customer-Centric Measures," *Marketing Management* 14, No. 4 (2005).

38. Frederick F. Reichheld, and W. Earl Sasser Jr., "Zero Defections: Quality Comes to Services," *Harvard Business Review* 68, No. 5 (September/October 1990), 105–111.

39. Harry Bacas, "Make It Right for the Customer," *Nation's Business*, 75 (November 1987), 49; and Charlotte Klopp and John Sterlicchi, "Customer Satisfaction Just Catching On in Europe," *Marketing News* 24, no. 11 (May 28, 1990), 5.

40. Joan C. Szabo, "Service = Survival," *Nation's Business* 77, no. 3 (March 1989), 16.

41. Patti Case, "City Company Makes Business Screening Firms for Consumers/Consumer Connections," *Journal Record*, May 16, 1987.

42. David Clutterbuck, "Developing Customer Care Training Programmes," *The International Journal of Bank Marketing* 10 (7) (1990) 17–21.

43. Christopher W. L. Hart, James L. Heskett, and W. Earl Sasser Jr., "The Profitable Art of Service Recovery," *Harvard Business Review* 68, no. 4 (July–August 1990), 148.

44. Tom Peters, *Thriving on Chaos* (New York: Alfred A. Knopf, 1988), 112.

45. Zabin and Brebach, *Precision Marketing*.

46. Timothy L. Keiningham, Tiffany Perkins-Munn, Lerzan Aksoy, and Demitry Estrin, "Does Customer Satisfaction Lead to Profitability? The Mediating Role of Share-of-Wallet," *Managing Service Quality* 15, No. 2 (2005), 172–181.

47. Werner Reinartz, and V. Kumar, "The Mismanagement of Customer Loyalty," *Harvard Business Review* 80, no. 7 (July 2002), 86–94.
48. Christopher Lovelock, and Evert Gummesson, "Whither Services Marketing: In Search of a New Paradigm and Fresh Perspectives," *Journal of Service Research* 7, no. 1 (August 2005), 20–41.
49. Kelly Kagamas Tomkies, "Banking on Service," *Smart Business Columbus* 12, no. 6 (March 1, 2004), 12.
50. Keiningham and Vavra, *The Customer Delight Principle*.
51. Philip K. Dick, quoted *I Hope I Shall Arrive Soon* (New York: St. Martin's Press, 1987).

CHAPTER 2 Loyalty Myths Contaminating Company Management Practices

1. Albert J. Dunlap, and Bob Andelman (1996) *Mean Business*. New York: Times Business.
2. Ibid., p. 4.
3. "Scott Paper Co.: Four-Step Program Restructures Operations," *Pulp & Paper*, December 1994, 34.
4. Charles Panati, *Panati's Extraordinary Origins of Everyday Things* (New York: Harper and Row, 1987), 205.
5. "Scott Paper Co.," *Pulp & Paper*.
6. Panati, *Panati's Extraordinary Origins of Everyday Things*.
7. Andrew Cassel, "After the Fall," *Across the Board*, April 1996, 31.
8. John A. Byrne, and Joseph Weber, "The Shredder: Did CEO Dunlap Save Scott Paper or Just Pretty It Up?" *Business Week*, January 15, 1996, 58.
9. "Scott Paper Co.," *Pulp & Paper*. Four-Step Program Restructures Operations," (December), 34.
10. Byrne and Weber, "The Shredder."
11. A. J. Vogl, "Tough Guy," *Across the Board*, February 1995, 16.
12. "Scott Paper Co.;" *Pulp & Paper*, Byrne and Weber, "The Shredder;" David Zimmerman, "Dunlap Chats About Chainsaw Ways," *USA Today*, August 30, 1996.
13. Debra Sparks, "Ming the Merciless," *Financial World*, June 1994, 26.
14. Cassel, "After the Fall."
15. Beth Reinhard, "Dunlap an Old Pro at Fixing Companies," *Palm Beach Post*, July 18, 1995.
16. Jonathan Burton, "Paper's Tiger," *Chief Executive*, March 1995, 36.
17. Donald Rumsfeld, "Downsizing Government," *Vital Speeches*, January 1, 1995.
18. David Zimmerman, "Dunlap Chats About Chainsaw Ways," *USA Today*, August 30, 1996.
19. Burton, "Paper's Tiger."
20. Vogl, "Tough Guy."
21. Byrne and Weber, "The Shredder."
22. Vogl, "Tough Guy."

23. Byrne and Weber, "The Shredder."
24. John A. Byrne, "The Making of a Corporate Tough Guy," *Business Week*, January 15, 1996, 61.
25. Vogl, "Tough Guy."
26. Byrne and Weber, "The Shredder."
27. Cassel, "After the Fall."
28. Byrne and Weber, "The Shredder."
29. Joseph Weber, "Scott Rolls Out a Risky Strategy," *Business Week*, May 22, 1995, 48.
30. Byrne and Weber, "The Shredder"; Randy Myers, "Why Scott Paper Dumped EVA," *CFO*, October 1995, 18.
31. Byrne and Weber, "The Shredder."
32. Jo Fleisher, "Duracell CEO Chides 'Rambo in Pinstripes,' " *Fairfield County Business Journal*, December 11, 1995.
33. Byrne and Weber, "The Shredder."
34. "1995 CEO of the Year Silver Award Winners," *Financial World*, March 28, 1995, 80.
35. Warren E. Buffett, *An Owner's Manual*, Omaha, NE: Berkshire Hathaway, Inc., 1996, www.berkshirehathaway.com.
36. Kevin F. Hallock, "Layoffs, Top Executive Pay, and Firm Performance," *The American Economic Review* 88, no. 4 (September 1998), 711–723; Oded Palmon, Huey-Lian Sun, and Alex P. Tang, "Layoff Announcements: Stock Market Impact and Financial Performance," *Financial Management* 26, no. 3 (Autumn 1997), 54–68.
37. Kevin P. Coyne, and Jonathon W. Witter, "Taking the Mystery Out of Investor Behavior," *Harvard Business Review*, September 2002, 68–78.
38. Jon A. Hilsenrath, "A Stock Theory Linking Price with Satisfaction Isn't Perfect," *Wall Street Journal*, February 19, 2003.
39. John A. Byrne, "The Horizontal Corporation," *Business Week*, December 20, 1993, 76; Rahul Jacob, and Rajiv M. Rao, "The Struggle to Create an Organization for the 21st Century," *Fortune* 131, no. 6 (April 3, 1995), 90.
40. Jacob and Rao, "The Struggle to Create an Organization for the 21st Century."
41. "Farewell to the Pyramid Chart," *Business Week*, December 20, 1993, 122.
42. Utpal M. Dholakia, and Vicki G. Morwitz, "The Scope and Persistence of Mere-Measurement Effects: Evidence from a Field Study of Customer Satisfaction Measurement," *Journal of Consumer Research*, 29, no. 2 (September 2002), 159–167.
43. Tony Kontzer, "Complete Customer Profiling Remains Elusive," *Information Week*, April 5, 2004, 67.
44. Gary Loveman, "Diamonds in the Data Mine," *Harvard Business Review* 81, no. 5 (May 2003), 109.
45. Ronald Henkoff, "Growing Your Company: Five Ways to Do It Right," *Fortune*, November 25, 1996, 81.
46. Gary L. Clark, Peter F. Kaminski, and David R. Rink, "Consumer Complaints: Advice on How Companies Should Respond," *The Journal of Consumer Marketing* 9, no. 3 (Summer 1992), 5–14.

47. Kent Grayson, and Tim Ambler, "The Dark Side of Long-Term Relationships in Marketing Services," *Journal of Marketing Research*, 36 (February 1999), 132–141; Christine Moorman, Gerald Zaltman, and Rohit Deshpandé, "Relationships between Providers and Users of Market Research: The Dynamics of Trust Between Organizations," *Journal of Marketing Research* 29 (August 1992), 314–328.

CHAPTER 3 Loyalty Myths about Customers: Their Needs, Behaviors, and Referrals

1. Siobhán Creaton, *Ryanair: How a Small Irish Airline Conquered Europe* (London: Aurum Press Ltd., 2004), 162.
2. James L. Heskett, Thomas O. Jones, Gary W. Loveman, W. Earl Sasser Jr., and Leonard A. Schlesinger, "Putting the Service-Profit Chain to Work," *Harvard Business Review* 72, No. 2 (March–April 1994), 164–174.
3. Steve Pain, "The Business Profile: Michael O'Leary—There will be only one low fares airline in Europe—Ryanair' cleared for take-off: But is the irrepressible Michael O'Leary flying too close to the sun?" *The Birmingham Post* (England), February 23, 2002.
4. Cathy Buyck, "Emulating Southwest (Ireland's Ryanair Holdings PLC pursues profits)," *Air Transport World*, September 1, 2000, and William Underhill, "Michael O'Leary (CEO of Ryanair Holdings PLC)," *Newsweek* (International), December 31, 2001.
5. Andrew Cave, "High Flier Who Built a Fortune on Low Fares; Saturday Profile Michael O'Leary Turned Round Ryanair—Now His Ambition Is to Make It the Biggest Airline in Europe," *Daily Telegraph* (London), August 10, 2002.
6. Glenn Frankel, "Ireland's Highflying Mr. Low Fare; Ryanair's O'Leary Built on the Southwest Example," *Washington Post*, March 5, 2004.
7. Creaton, *Ryanair*.
8. Ibid.
9. Daniel McGinn, "Is This Any Way to Run an Airline?" *Newsweek*, October 4, 2004.
10. Creaton, *Ryanair*.
11. Glenn Frankel, "Ireland's Highflying Mr. Low Fare."
12. Jeff Randall, "Ryanair is Heading for a Nose Dive," *Sunday Telegraph* (London), June 23, 2002.
13. Keith Johnson, "Budget Airlines Seek Bigger Review Bite with 'Some Frills'," *Wall Street Journal*, October 5, 2004, B1.
14. McGinn, "Is This Any Way to Run an Airline?"
15. Robert M. Kahn, "Stocking a Positive Retail Experience," *The Boston Herald*, March 24, 1997.
16. James R. Rosenfield, "The Hidden Dangers of Relationship Marketing," *Direct*, October 1, 1994.
17. Andrew S.C. Ehrenberg, and Gerald J. Goodhardt, *Understanding Buyer Behavior* (New York: J. Walter Thompson and the Market Research Corporation of America, 1977).

18. Grahame R. Dowling, and Mark Uncles, "Do Customer Loyalty Programs Really Work?" *Sloan Management Review*, 38, no. 4 (Summer 1997), 71–82.
19. TARP, *Consumer Complaint Handling in America: An Update Study* (Washington, DC: White House Office of Consumer Affairs, 1986).
20. Roland T. Rust, Katherine N. Lemon, and Valarie A. Zeithaml, "Return on Marketing: Using Customer Equity to Focus Marketing Strategy," *Journal of Marketing* 68, No. 1 (January 2004), 109–127.
21. Thomas O. Jones, and W. Earl Sasser Jr., "Why Satisfied Customers Defect" and "Apostles and Terrorists: A Company's Best Friends and Worst Enemies," *Harvard Business Review*, 73, no. 6 (November/December 1995), 88–99.
22. Allan L. Baldinger, Edward Blair, and Raj Echambadi, "Why Brands Grow," *Journal of Advertising Research*, 42, no. 1 (January/February 2002), 7–14.
23. Philip Stern, and Kathy Hammond, "The Relationship Between Customer Loyalty and Purchase Incidence," *Marketing Letters* 15, no. 1, (2004), 5–19.
24. Andrew S.C. Ehrenberg, Mark D. Uncles, and Gerald J. Goodhardt, "Understanding Brand Performance Measures: Using Dirichlet Benchmarks, *Journal of Business Research* 57, no. 12 (December 2004), 1307–1325.
25. Stern and Hammond, "The Relationship Between Customer Loyalty and Purchase Incidence."
26. Kevin J. Clancy, "Save America's Dying Brands," *Marketing Management*, 10, no. 3 (September/October 2001), 36–44.
27. "Survey Shows Over-50s Feel Alienated by Ads," *Marketing Week*, (London) October 21, 2004, 9.
28. Bob Moos, "Advertisers Try to Appeal to Over-50 Boomers," *Knight Ridder Tribune Business News* (Washington, DC), October 31, 2004, 1.
29. TARP, *Consumer Complaint Handling in America*.
30. Frederick F. Reichheld, and W. Earl Sasser Jr., "Zero Defections: Quality Comes to Services," *Harvard Business Review* 68, no. 5 (September/October 1990), 105–111.
31. Eugene W. Anderson, "Customer Satisfaction and Word-of-Mouth," *Journal of Service Research* 1, no. 1 (August 1998), 1–14.
32. Geok Theng Lau, and Sophia Ng, "Individual and Situational Factors Influencing Negative Word-of-Mouth Behaviour," *Canadian Journal of Administrative Sciences* 18, no. 3, (2001), 163–178.
33. Werner Reinartz, and V. Kumar, "The Mismanagement of Customer Loyalty," *Harvard Business Review* 80, no. 7 (July 2002), 86–94.
34. Frederick F. Reichheld, "The One Number You Need to Grow," *Harvard Business Review* 81, no. 12 (December 2003), 46.
35. Source: www.creativequotations.com.
36. Ruth N. Bolton, and James H. Drew, "A Longitudinal Analysis of the Impact of Service Changes on Customer Attitudes," *Journal of Marketing* 55, no. 1, (January 1991), 1–10; William Boulding, Ajay Kalra, Richard Staelin, and Valarie A. Zeithaml, "A Dynamic Process Model of Service Quality," *Journal of Marketing Research* 30, no. 1 (February 1993), 7–27; Piyush Kumar, "The Impact of Performance, Cost, and Competitive Considerations on the Relationship between Satisfaction and Repurchase Intent in Business Markets," *Journal of Service Re-*

search 5, no. 1 (August 2002), 55–68; Priscilla A. LaBarbera, and David Mazursky, "A Longitudinal Assessment of Consumer Satisfaction/Dissatisfaction: The Dynamic Aspect of the Cognitive Process," *Journal of Marketing Research* 20, no. 4 (November 1983), 393–404; Vikas Mittal, Pankaj Kumar, and Michael Tsiros, "Attribute-Level Performance, Satisfaction, and Behavioral Intentions over Time: A Consumption-System Approach," *Journal of Marketing* 63, no. 2 (April 1999), 88–101; Vikas Mittal, William T. Ross Jr., and Patrick M. Baldasare, "The Asymmetric Impact of Negative and Positive Attribute-Level Performance on Overall Satisfaction and Repurchase Intentions," *Journal of Marketing* 62, no. 1 (January 1998), 33–47; Richard L. Oliver, and Wayne DeSarbo, "Response Determinants in Satisfaction Judgments," *Journal of Consumer Research* 14, no. 4 (March 1988), 495–507.

37. Eugene W. Anderson, and Mary W. Sullivan, "The Antecedents and Consequences of Customer Satisfaction for Firms," *Marketing Science* 12 (Spring 1993), 125–143; Ruth N. Bolton, "A Dynamic Model of the Duration of the Customer's Relationship with a Continuous Service Provider: The Role of Satisfaction," *Marketing Science* 17, no. 1 (1998), 45–65; Christopher Ittner, and David F. Larcker, "Are Non-financial Measures Leading Indicators of Financial Performance? An Analysis of Customer Satisfaction," *Journal of Accounting Research* 36 (Supplement), (1998), 1–35; Jones and Sasser, "Why Satisfied Customers Defect"; Gary W. Loveman, "Employee Satisfaction, Customer Loyalty, and Financial Performance: An Empirical Examination of the Service-Profit Chain in Retail Banking," *Journal of Service Research* 1, no. 1 (August 1998), 18–31; Vikas Mittal, and Wagner Kamakura, "Satisfaction, Repurchase Intent, and Repurchase Behavior: Investigating the Moderating Effect of Customer Characteristics," *Journal of Marketing Research* 38 (February 2001), 131–142.

38. Eugene W. Anderson, and Claes Fornell, "The Customer Satisfaction Index as a Leading Indicator," *Handbook of Services Marketing and Management*, Teresa A. Swartz and Dawn Iacobucci, eds., (Thousand Oaks, CA: Sage 1994), 255–267; Eugene W. Anderson, Claes Fornell, and Donald R. Lehmann, "Customer Satisfaction, Market Share, and Profitability: Findings from Sweden," *Journal of Marketing* 58 (July 1994), 53–66; Eugene W. Anderson, Claes Fornell, and Roland T. Rust, "Customer Satisfaction, Productivity, and Profitability: Differences between Goods and Services," *Marketing Science* 16, no. 2 (1997), 129–145; Eugene W. Anderson and Vikas Mittal, "Strengthening the Satisfaction-Profit Chain," *Journal of Service Research* 3, no. 2 (November 2000), 107–120; Kenneth L. Bernhardt, Naveen Donthu, and Pamela A. Kennett, "A Longitudinal Analysis of Satisfaction and Profitability," *Journal of Business Research* 47, no. 2 (February 2000), 161–171; Claes Fornell, Michael D. Johnson, Eugene W. Anderson, Jaesung Cha, and Barbara Everitt Bryant, "The American Customer Satisfaction Index: Nature, Purpose, and Findings," *Journal of Marketing* 60, no. 4 (October 1996), 7–18; Eugene C. Nelson, Roland T. Rust, Anthony Zahorik, Robin L. Rose, Paul Batalden, and Beth Ann Siemanski, "Do Patient Perceptions of Quality Relate to Hospital Financial Performance," *Marketing Health Services* 12, no. 4 (December 1992), 6–13; Roland T. Rust, and Anthony J. Zahorik, "Customer Satisfaction, Customer Retention, and Market Share," *Journal of Retailing* 69, no. 2 (Summer 1993), 193–215.

39. Eugene W. Anderson, "Customer Satisfaction and Word-of-Mouth," *Journal of Service Research* 1, no. 1 (August 1998), 1–14; A. Parasuraman, Leonard L. Berry, and Valarie A. Zeithaml, "Refinement and Reassessment of the SERVQUAL Scale," *Journal of Retailing* 67, no. 4 (Winter 1991), 420–450; A. Parasuraman, Valarie A. Zeithaml, and Leonard L. Berry, "SERVQUAL: A Multiple-Item Scale for Measuring Consumer Perceptions of Service Quality," *Journal of Retailing* 64, no. 1 (Spring 1988), 12–40.
40. Eugene W. Anderson, Claes Fornell, and Sanal K. Mazvancheryl, "Customer Satisfaction and Shareholder Value," *Journal of Marketing* 68, no. 4, (October 2004), 172–185; "The ACSI, Predictive Capabilities," http://www.theacsi.org/predictive_capabilities.htm.
41. Devon Spurgeon, "In Return to Power, the Nordstrom Family Finds a Pile of Problems—A Father and Son Must Chart New Course after a Fling with Halters and Hip-Hop, *Wall Street Journal*, September 8, 2000, B1.

CHAPTER 4   Loyalty Myths Concerning Loyalty Programs

1. A statement from Mr. Servet Topaloğlu, November 12, 2004.
2. Author interview with Mr. Bora Tanrıkulu, marketing manager, and Ms. Çiler Tüzüner, marketing and communications specialist, Tansaş Headquarters, Istanbul, Turkey, November 12, 2004.
3. Tansaş financial statements, end of fiscal year 2004.
4. James Cigiliano, Margaret Georgiadis, Darren Pleasance, and Susan Whalley, "The Price of Loyalty," *McKinsey Quarterly*, Issue 4, 2000.
5. G. Dowling, "Customer Relationship Management: In B2C Markets, Often Less Is More," *California Management Review* 44, no. 3, (2000), 87–104.
6. B. Sharp, and A. Sharp, "Loyalty Programs and Their Impact on Repeat-Purchase Loyalty Patterns," *International Journal of Research in Marketing* 14, no. 5 (December 1997), 473-486.
7. WebFlyer, "LatinPass Laws," April 1, 2002.
8. *New York Times*, "Joining the Million Mile Club," June 25, 2000.
9. Mary A. Dempsey, "Requiem for a Free Seat," *Latin Trade* 8, no. 11 (November 1, 2000), 56.
10. Richard L. Oliver, "Whence Customer Loyalty," *Journal of Marketing* 63 (Special issue) (1999), 33–44.
11. R.N. Bolton, P.K. Kannan, and M.D. Bramlet, "Implications of Loyalty Program Membership and Service Experiences for Customer Retention and Value," *Journal of the Academy of Marketing Science* 28, no. 1 (Winter 2000), 95–108.
12. C. Wright, and L. Sparks, "Loyalty Saturation in Retailing: Exploring the End of Retail Loyalty Cards?" *International Journal of Retail & Distribution Management* 27, Issue 10/11 (1999), 429–439.
13. Mark D. Uncles, Grahame R. Dowling, and Kathy Hammond (2003), "Customer Loyalty and Customer Loyalty Programs," *Journal of Consumer Marketing*, 20 (4), 294–316.

14. *PR Newswire*, "Loyalty program defection increases when rewards are slow; Maritz Loyalty Marketing reveals top reasons customers leave and recommends strategies to keep them," September 14, 2004.
15. Ibid.
16. *USA Today*, "Mileage Maniacs Say the Real Fun Is in the Game," May 19, 2000.
17. Mary A. Dempsey, "Requiem for a Free Seat," *Latin Trade* 8, no. 11 (November 1, 2000), 56.
18. Techmark web site: http://www.loyaltymarketing.com/loyalty.html (accessed December 2, 2004).
19. Webloyalty.com web site: http://www.webloyalty.com/partnerad.asp?ref=overture loyaltyprogram (accessed December 2, 2004).
20. Repeat Rewards web site: http://www.repeatrewards.com/loyalty.html (accessed December 2, 2004).
21. Dempsey, "Requiem for a Free Seat."
22. *Chicago Tribune*, "20 Years of Miles—With Trillions to Burn," May 13, 2001.
23. Roger Collis, "The Price of Success: Mileage Plans Losing Their Luster," *International Herald Tribune*, May 23, 1997.
24. *USA Today*, "How Far Would You Go for a Million Miles?" May 19, 2000.
25. John G. Lynch, and Dan Ariely, "Wine Online: Search Costs Affect Competition on Price, Quality, and Distribution," *Marketing Science* 19, no. 1 (Winter 2000), 83.
26. Kristin Diehl, Laura Kornish, and John G. Lynch, "Smart Agents: When Lower Search Costs for Quality Information Increase Price Sensitivity," *Journal of Consumer Research* 30, no. 1 (June 2003), 56.
27. Frederick F. Reichheld, and Phil Schefter, "E-Loyalty: Your Secret Weapon on the Web" *Harvard Business Review* 78, no. 4 (July–August 2000), 105.
28. Beth Negus Vivieros, "Invited Guests: Leading Hotels Uses Exclusivity to Book Members for Loyalty Program," *Direct*, December 2004, 39–42.
29. Louise O'Brien, and Charles Jones, "Do Rewards Really Create Loyalty?" *Harvard Business Review* 73, no. 3 (May 1995), 75.

CHAPTER 5   Loyalty Myths about Loyalty, Share of Business, and Profitability

1. *Fair Disclosure Wire*, "Best Buy Co., Inc. at Banc of America Securities Consumer Conference—Final," April 1, 2004.
2. Gail Edmondson, "The Taming of France Télécom; Michel Bon Soothed Labor and Has Privatization on Track," *Business Week*, January 27, 1997, 18.
3. *The Economist*, "France Télécom: The Picket Line," 336, no. 7932 (September 16, 1995), 74–75.
4. Ibid.
5. Edmondson, "The Taming of France Télécom."
6. *CNN.com*, "Bon Calls Time on Tenure," September 13, 2002.
7. Ibid.
8. Edmondson, "The Taming of France Télécom."

9. *CNN.com*, "Bon Calls Time on Tenure."
10. Carol Matlack and Stanley Reed, "France Télécom's $53 Billion Burden," *Business Week* (international edition), January 8, 2001.
11. Didier Pouillot, "The Changing Culture of French Telecoms," *Telecommunications*, 31, no. 5 (May, 1997), 31.
12. Carol Matlack, "France Télécom: Now the Hunting Begins; With Its Deutsche Telekom Link Unraveling, It's Chasing Deals," *Business Week*, August 2, 1999, 16.
13. Ibid.
14. *Business Wire*, "France Telecom 1999 Financial Results: Strong Growth in New Business Areas," March 1, 2000.
15. *CNN Money*, "France Télécom's 'Bon' Deal," May 31, 2000.
16. Jo Johnson, "The French Exceptions," *Financial Times*, June 28, 2002.
17. *CNN.com*, (Europe), "France Tel Chief Pulls Plug," September 13, 2002.
18. Janet Guyon, "France Télécom's Debt Glut: CEO Michel Bon May Soon Find Investors Demanding His Head," *Fortune*, March 7, 2002.
19. Andy Reinhardt, Stephen Baker, and Carol Matlack, "France Inc. Follies; Two of Its High-Profile Companies Find Themselves in Deep Trouble," *Business Week*, July 8, 2002, 48.
20. Andy Reinhardt, France Télécom: Such Promise, but Zut Alors! Such Debt," *Business Week*, October 7, 2002, 74.
21. Guyon, "France Télécom's Debt Glut."
22. Kevin J. Delaney, "France Télécom CEO Defies 'Attack'—Amid Rating Downgrades, Bon Says Issuance of Shares Isn't Needed to Raise Cash," *Wall Street Journal*, June 26, 2002, B14.
23. *CNN.com* (Europe), "France Tel Chief Pulls Plug," September 13, 2002.
24. Blaine Greteman, "France Télécom Says Bon Voyage," *Time* (Europe) 160, no. 13 (September 23, 2002).
25. John Rossant, Jason Bush, Kerry Capell, Laura Cohn, Gail Edmondson, Jack Ewing, David Fairlamb, et al, "Stars of Europe: 25 Leaders at the Forefront of Change," *Business Week*, June 7, 2004.
26. Pierre Tran, "France Telecom Rushes in New Top Man," *Knight Ridder Tribune Business News*, March 2, 2005, 1.
27. *New York Times*, "Amid Overhaul, France Telecom Selects New Chief," February 28, 2005, C3.
28. *The Economist*, "Europe: Breton to the Rescue; France's Finance Minister," 374, no. 8416 (March 5, 2005), 40.
29. *New York Times*, "Amid Overhaul, France Telecom Selects New Chief."
30. William Finnie and Robert M Randall, "Loyalty as a Philosophy and Strategy: An Interview with Frederick F. Reichheld," *Strategy & Leadership* 30, no. 2 (2002), 25–31.
31. Werner Reinartz, and V. Kumar, "On the Profitability of Long-Life Customers in a Noncontractual Setting: An Empirical Investigation and Implications for Marketing," *Journal of Marketing* 64, no. 4 (October 2000), 17–35.
32. Reinartz and Kumar, "On the Profitability of Long-Life Customers"; W. Reinartz and V. Kumar, "The Mismanagement of Customer Loyalty," *Harvard Business Review* 80, no. 7 (July 2002), 86–94.

33. Finnie and Randall, "Loyalty as a Philosophy and Strategy."
34. Reinartz and Kumar, "On the Profitability of Long-Life Customers and "The Mismanagement of Customer Loyalty."
35. Dina El Boghdady, "Giving Discounts Where It Counts; More Retailers Using Coupons to Lure Biggest Spenders," *Washington Post*, December 19, 2003.
36. George Stalk Jr., and Thomas M. Hout, *Competing Against Time: How Time-Based Competition Is Reshaping Global Markets*, (New York: The Free Press, 1990), 5–6.
37. W. Edwards Deming, *Out of the Crisis* (Boston: MIT Center for Advanced Engineering Study, 1986); J.M. Juran, and Frank M. Gryna Jr., *Quality Planning and Analysis: From Product Development through Use* (New York: McGraw-Hill, 1986).
38. Finnie and Randall, "Loyalty as a Philosophy and Strategy."
39. Frederick F. Reichheld, and W. Earl Sasser Jr., "Zero Defections: Quality Comes to Services," *Harvard Business Review* 68, no. 5 (September/October 1990), 106.
40. Reinartz and Kumar, "On the Profitability of Long-Life Customers" and "The Mismanagement of Customer Loyalty."
41. Robert. S. Kaplan and V.G. Narayanan, *Customer Profitability Measurement and Management*, white paper, Inc.: Houston, TX: Acorn Systems, May 2001) http://www.acornsys.com/value/whitepapers/WP-CustomerProfitabilityMM.html.
42. Mark D. Uncles, Grahame R. Dowling, and Kathy Hammond, "Customer Loyalty and Customer Loyalty Programs," *Journal of Consumer Marketing* 20, no. 4 (2003), 294–316.
43. *Direct Marketing*, "Consumers Say 'No Thanks' to Relationships with Brands," 64, no. 1 (May 2001), 48–55.

CHAPTER 6   Loyalty Myths Regarding Employees

1. Michael Liedtke, "Michael Liedtke Column," *Contra Costa Times* (Walnut Creek, CA), September 13, 1998.
2. Bill Ritter, "The Safeway Smile," *ABC 20-20*, October 30, 1998, transcript of television program.
3. Elaine Korry and Daniel Zwerdling, *Weekend All Things Considered*, September 27, 1998.
4. *Business Wire* (1998), "Safeway Employees Announce the Filing of a Charge with the Equal Employment Opportunity Commission," November 16, 1998.
5. Ibid.
6. Ritter, "The Safeway Smile."
7. Liedtke, "Michael Liedtke Column."
8. James L. Heskett, Thomas O. Jones, Gary W. Loveman, W. Earl Sasser Jr., and Leonard A. Schlesinger, "Putting the Service-Profit Chain to Work," *Harvard Business Review* 72, no. 2 (March–April, 1994), 164–174.
9. Roland T. Rust, Anthony J. Zahorik, and Timothy L. Keiningham, *Return on Quality: Measuring the Financial Impact of Your Company's Quest for Quality* (Chicago: Irwin Professional Publishing, 1994), xv.
10. Walter Kichell III, "How Important Is Morale, Really?" *Fortune* 119, no. 4 (February 13, 1989), 121–122.

11. Timothy L. Keiningham, Lerzan Aksoy, Kenneth Peterson, and Terry G. Vavra, "The Asymmetric Impact of Employee and Customer Satisfaction on Retail Sales: An Examination of Changes in Customer and Employee Perceptions, and the Consistency of These Perceptions," Istanbul, Turkey: KOÇ University working paper, 2004.

12. Bruce Pfau, "Employee Commitment Goes Hand-in-Hand with Shareholder Value," *St. Louis Post-Dispatch*, February 1, 2000, B1.

13. Birgit Benkhoff, "Ignoring Commitment Is Costly: New Approaches Establish the Missing Link Between Commitment and Performance," *Human Relations* 5, no. 6 (1997), 701–726; Richard T. Mowday, Layman W. Porter, and Richard M. Steers, *Employee Organization Linkages* (New York: Academic Press, 1982).

14. John E. Mathieu and D. Zajac, "A Review and Meta-Analysis of the Antecedents, Correlates and Consequences of Organizational Commitment and Job Performance: It's the Nature of the Commitment that Counts," *Psychological Bulletin* 108, no. 2 (1990), p. 184.

15. Roger Hallowell and Leonard A. Schlesinger, "The Service-Profit Chain: Intellectual Roots, Current Realities, and Future Prospects," in *Handbook of Services Marketing & Management*, Teresa A. Swartz and Dawn Iacobucci, eds. (Thousand Oaks, CA: Sage Publications, 2000).

16. Lisa Salters and Aaron Brown, *ABC Good Morning America*, September 27, 1998.

17. Douglas M. McGregor, *The Human Side of Enterprise* (New York: McGraw-Hill, 1960).

18. Marcus Buckingham and Curt Coffman, *First, Break All the Rules* (New York: Simon & Schuster, 1999).

19. Benjamin Schneider and David E. Bowen, *Winning the Service Game* (Boston: Harvard Business School Press, 1995).

CHAPTER 7   The Foundations of Customer Loyalty

1. Frederick F. Reichheld, *The Loyalty Effect* (Boston: Harvard Business School Press, 1996).

2. R.L. Oliver, *Satisfaction: A Behavioral Perspective on the Consumer* (New York: Irwin/McGraw-Hill, 1997).

3. Melvin Thomas Copeland, "Relation of Consumers' Buying Habits to Marketing Methods," *Harvard Business Review* 1, no. 1 (April 1923), 282–289.

4. Jacob Jacoby and Robert W. Chestnut, *Brand Loyalty Measurement and Management* (New York: John Wiley & Sons, 1978).

5. G.H. Brown, "Brown Clarifies Share-of-Market Figures in Brand Loyalty," *Journal of Marketing* 17 (1953), 304.

6. James R. Bettman, Mary Frances Luce, and John W. Payne, "Constructive Consumer Choice Processes," *Journal of Consumer Research* 25, no. 3 (December 1998), 187–217.

7. Ibid.

8. Mark D. Uncles, Grahame R. Dowling, and Kathy Hammond, "Customer Loyalty and Customer Loyalty Programs," *Journal of Consumer Marketing* 20, No. 4 (2004).

9. John Howard, *Consumer Behavior in Marketing Strategy* (Englewood Cliffs, NJ: Prentice-Hall, 1989).
10. Australian Broadcasting Corporation's official *Fat Cow Motel* web site: http://www.fatcowmotel.com.au
11. Australian Broadcasting Corporation's media release: http://www.abc.net.au/corp/pubs/s1001843.htm
12. "The Global Brand Scoreboard: The 100 Top Brands," *Business Week*, August 2, 2004, 68–71.
13. Timothy L. Keiningham, Lerzan Aksoy, Tiffany Perkins-Munn, and Terry Vavra, "The Convergence of Customer Centric and Brand Centric Measures," *Marketing Management* 14, No. 4 (2005).
14. Robert M. McMath, "The Perils of Typecasting," *American Demographics* 19, no. 2, (February 1997), 60.
15. H. Simon, " A Behavioral Model of Rational Choice," *Quarterly Journal of Economics* 69 (February 1995), 99–118.
16. Bettman et al., "Constructive Consumer Choice Processes."
17. Itamar Simonson, "Shoppers Easily Influenced in Choices," *New York Times*, November 6, 1994.
18. Susan Fournier, "Consumers and Their Brands: Developing Relationship Theory in Consumer Research," *Journal of Consumer Research* 24, No. 4 (March 1998), 343–373.
19. Mark D. Uncles, Grahame R. Dowling, and Kathy Hammond, "Customer Loyalty and Customer Loyalty Programs," *Journal of Consumer Marketing* 20 (4), 294–316.
20. Arthur M. Hughes, "Boosting Reponse with RFM," *Marketing Tools*, (May 1996), 4–10.
21. J.R. Miglautsch, "Application of R-F-M Principles: What to Do with 1-1-1 Customers?" *Journal of Database Marketing*, 9, no. 4 (July 2002), 319–324.

CHAPTER 8 The Right Way to Manage for Customer Loyalty

1. V. Kumar is the ING Chair Professor at the University of Connecticut's School of Business in Storrs, Connecticut, where he is also executive director of the ING Center for Financial Services. Roland T. Rust is the David Bruce Smith Chair in Marketing at the Robert H. Smith School of Business at the University of Maryland in College Park, Maryland, where he serves as executive director of the Center for Excellence in Service. He assumed editorship of the *Journal of Marketing* in 2005.
2. Source: http://www.jkdwomen.com/.
3. Oscar Wilde (1854–1900), Anglo-Irish playwright, author; spoken by the character Algernon in *The Importance of Being Earnest*, Act 1.
4. Isaac Asimov, "The Relativity of Wrong," *The Skeptical Inquirer* 14, no. 1 (Fall 1989), 35–44, http://chem.tufts.edu/AnswersInScience/RelativityofWrong.htm.
5. V. Kumar and Denish Shah, "Building and Sustaining Profitable Customer Loyalty for the 21st Century," *Journal of Retailing* 80, no. 4 (Winter 2004), 317–330.
6. Paul D. Berger, and Nada I. Nasr, "Customer Lifetime Value: Marketing Models and Applications," *Journal of Interactive Marketing* 12 (Winter 1998), 17–30.

7. R. Venkatesan, and V. Kumar, "A Customer Lifetime Value Framework for Customer Selection and Resource Allocation Strategy," *Journal of Marketing* 68, no. 4 (October 2004), 106–125.
8. Werner J. Reinartz and V. Kumar, "On the Profitability of Long-Life Customers in a Noncontractual Setting: An Empirical Investigation and Implications for Marketing." *Journal of Marketing* 64 no. 4 (October 2000), 17–35.
9. META Group, "Industry Overview: New Insights in Data Warehousing Solutions," *Information Week*, 1996, 1–27HP.
10. Emmy Favilla, "Who's Who in CRM: Oracle CEO Larry Ellison Tops a List of Dynamic Leaders Driving the CRM Industry Forward," *CRM Magazine*, May 1, 2004.
11. Kumar and Shah, "Building and Sustaining Profitable Customer Loyalty for the 21st Century."
12. Timothy Keiningham and Terry Vavra, *The Customer Delight Principle* (New York: McGraw-Hill and the American Marketing Association, 2002).
13. W. Reinartz, J. Thomas, and V. Kumar, "Balancing Acquisition and Retention Resources to Maximize Profitability," *Journal of Marketing*, 69, no. 1 (January 2005), 3–79.
14. Benjamin Schneider and David E. Bowen, *Winning the Service Game* (Boston: Harvard Business School Press, 1995).
15. R. Rust, T. Ambler, G. Carpenter, V. Kumar, and R. Srivastava, "Measuring Marketing Productivity: Current Knowledge and Future Directions," *Journal of Marketing* 68, no. 4 (October 2004), 76–89.
16. Roland T. Rust, Valerie A. Zeithaml, and Katherine N. Lemon, *Driving Customer Equity: How Customer Lifetime Value is Reshaping Corporate Strategy* (New York: The Free Press, 2000). See also two articles by the same authors: "Return on Marketing: Using Customer Equity to Focus Marketing Strategy," *Journal of Marketing*, 68, no. 1 (January 2004), 109–127 and "Customer-Centered Brand Management, *Harvard Business Review* 82, no. 9 (September 2004), 110–118.
17. Werner Reinartz and V. Kumar, "The Mismanagement of Customer Loyalty," *Harvard Business Review*, July 2002, 86–94.

INDEX